GRADE

PHONICS

SPECTRUM
Columbus, Ohio

Index of Skills

Phonics Grade 1

Numerals indicate the exercise pages on which these skills appear.

Auditory Skills

Associate sounds with letters—all activities

Discriminate initial sounds—6, 7, 8, 9, 10, 11, 12, 13, 14, 15, 20, 23, 82, 83, 84, 85, 86, 87, 88, 89, 90, 91, 92, 93, 94, 95, 96, 100, 113, 114, 115, 116, 121, 122

Discriminate final sounds—16, 17, 18, 19, 20, 97, 98, 99, 100, 117, 118, 119, 120, 121, 122

Discriminate vowel sounds—21, 22, 23, 25, 26, 29, 30, 31, 34, 35, 38, 39, 40, 43, 44, 45, 48, 49, 50, 51, 52, 53, 55, 56, 57, 58, 59, 60, 61, 62, 63, 64, 65, 66, 67, 68, 69, 70, 71, 72, 73, 75, 76, 77, 78, 79, 80, 81, 101, 102, 103, 104, 105, 106, 107, 108, 109, 110, 111, 112

Following directions—all activities

Recognize rhyming words—50, 54, 59, 69, 103

Visual Skills

Discriminate letters—6, 7, 8, 9, 10, 11, 12, 13, 14, 15, 17, 18, 46, 73, 118

Discriminate pictures/identify objects—6, 7, 8, 9, 10, 11, 12, 13, 14, 15, 16, 17, 18, 19, 20, 21, 22, 23, 24, 25, 26, 27, 28, 29, 30, 31, 32, 33, 34, 35, 36, 37, 38, 39, 40, 41, 42, 43, 44, 45, 47, 48, 49, 50, 51, 52, 53, 54, 55, 56, 57, 58, 59, 60, 61, 62, 63, 64, 65, 66, 67, 68, 69, 70, 71, 72, 73, 75, 76, 78, 80, 81, 82, 83, 84, 85, 86, 87, 88, 89, 91, 92, 93, 94, 95, 96, 97, 98, 99, 100, 101, 102, 103, 104, 105, 106, 107, 108, 109, 110, 112, 113, 114, 115, 116, 117, 118, 119, 120, 122

Discriminate words—23, 24, 27, 28, 32, 33, 36, 37, 41, 42, 43, 45, 49, 51, 53, 54, 55, 56, 58, 59, 60, 62, 63, 64, 65, 67, 68, 69, 71, 72, 75, 76, 77, 78, 80, 81, 84, 85, 86, 89, 90, 91, 96, 99, 100, 101, 102, 103, 104, 105, 106, 107, 109, 110, 111, 112, 114, 115, 116, 120, 121, 122

Writing Skills

Write letters—6, 7, 8, 9, 10, 11, 12, 13, 14, 15, 20, 22, 26, 29, 31, 35, 38, 40, 44, 66, 84, 85, 89, 94, 95, 98, 105, 115, 119

Write words—24, 28, 33, 37, 42, 45, 50, 51, 54, 55, 56, 59, 60, 63, 64, 65, 68, 69, 71, 72, 76, 78, 79, 80, 81, 86, 91, 96, 99, 100, 102, 103, 104, 108, 109, 110, 112, 116, 122

Write sentences—79, 109, 110, 116, 118

Consonant Letters and Sounds

b—6, 17	n—11
c—6	p—11, 18
d—7, 17	q—12
f—7, 17	r—12, 18
g—8, 18	s—13, 18
h—8	t—13, 18
j—9	v—14
k—9, 17	w—14
l—10	y—15
m—10, 17	z—15

Short Vowels

a—21, 22, 23, 29, 43, 44, 45, 46, 47, 49, 75, 76, 77, 78, 80, 81

e—25, 26, 27, 28, 29, 43, 44, 45, 46, 47, 75, 76, 77, 78, 80

i—30, 31, 32, 33, 38, 43, 44, 45, 46, 47, 53, 75, 76, 77, 78, 80, 81

o—34, 35, 36, 37, 38, 43, 44, 45, 46, 47, 58, 75, 76, 77, 78, 80

u—39, 40, 41, 42, 43, 44, 45, 46, 47, 62, 75, 76, 77, 78, 80, 81

Long Vowels

a—48, 49, 50, 51, 56, 66, 67, 68, 69, 70, 71, 72, 73, 74, 75, 76, 77, 78, 80, 81, 101, 103, 112

e—102, 103, 112

i—52, 53, 54, 55, 56, 66, 67, 68, 69, 70, 71, 72, 73, 74, 75, 76, 77, 78, 80, 81

o—57, 58, 59, 60, 65, 66, 67, 68, 69, 70, 71, 72, 73, 74, 75, 76, 77, 78, 80, 104, 108, 112

u—61, 62, 63, 64, 65, 66, 67, 68, 69, 70, 71, 72, 73, 74, 75, 76, 77, 78, 80, 81

y—109, 110, 111, 112

Other Vowel Sounds

oo—105, 106, 107, 108, 112

Consonant Blends

82, 83, 84, 85, 86, 87, 88, 89, 90, 91, 92, 93, 94, 95, 96, 97, 98, 99, 100

Consonant Pairs

113, 114, 115, 116, 117, 118, 119, 120, 121, 122

Table of Contents

Text Copyright © 2007 School Specialty Publishing. Published by Spectrum, an imprint of School Specialty Publishing, a member of the School Specialty Family.
Art Copyright © 2001 Mercer Mayer.

LITTLE CRITTER, MERCER MAYER'S LITTLE CRITTER and MERCER MAYER'S LITTLE CRITTER and logo are registered trademarks of Orchard House Licensing Company. All rights reserved.

A Big Tuna Trading Company, LLC/J.R. Sansevere Book
Printed in the United States of America. All rights reserved. Except as permitted under the United States Copyright Act, no part of this publication may be reproduced or distributed in any form or by any means, or stored in a database retrieval system, without prior written permission from the publisher.

Send all inquiries to: School Specialty Publishing, 8720 Orion Place, Columbus OH 43240-2111

ISBN 0-7696-8071-2

5 6 7 8 9 10 WAL 10 09

WELCOME TO CRITTERVILLE!

Spider

Frog

Grasshopper

Mouse

Little Critter

Little Sister

Dad

Kitty

Mom

Blue

Gator

Bat Child

Gabby

Bun Bun

Tiger

Maurice

Molly

Malcolm

Consonants Review: B and C

Directions: Say the name of each picture. Circle the letter that shows the beginning sound of each picture name.

c r b	b c t	p s c
b s k	c d n	w b t

Directions: Say the name of each picture. Write the letter that shows the beginning sound of each picture name.

_____   _____   _____

- - - - -   - - - - -   - - - - -

_____   _____   _____

Name _____

Consonants Review: D and F

Directions: Say the name of each picture. Circle the letter that shows the beginning sound of each picture name.

f g h	b f x	c h d
c d k	s m d	f n p

Directions: Say the name of each picture. Write the letter that shows the beginning sound of each picture name.

Consonants Review: G and H

Directions: Say the name of each picture. Circle the letter that shows the beginning sound of each picture name.

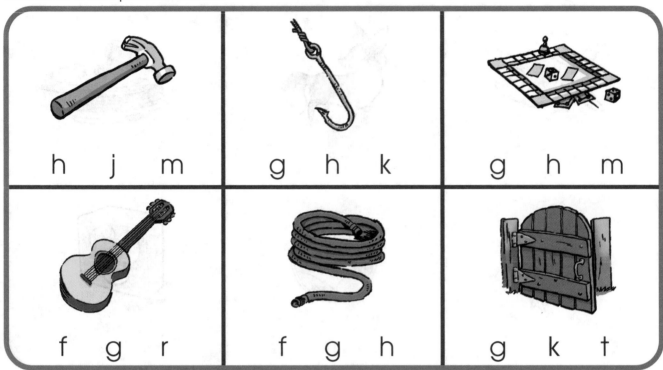

h j m	g h k	g h m
f g r	f g h	g k t

Directions: Say the name of each picture. Write the letter that shows the beginning sound of each picture name.

_____   _____   _____

Consonants Review: J and K

Directions: Say the name of each picture. Circle the letter that shows the beginning sound of each picture name.

k l m	h j r	k g r
t v j	h k t	g r k

Directions: Say the name of each picture. Write the letter that shows the beginning sound of each picture name.

_____   _____   _____

Consonants Review: L and M

Directions: Say the name of each picture. Circle the letter that shows the beginning sound of each picture name.

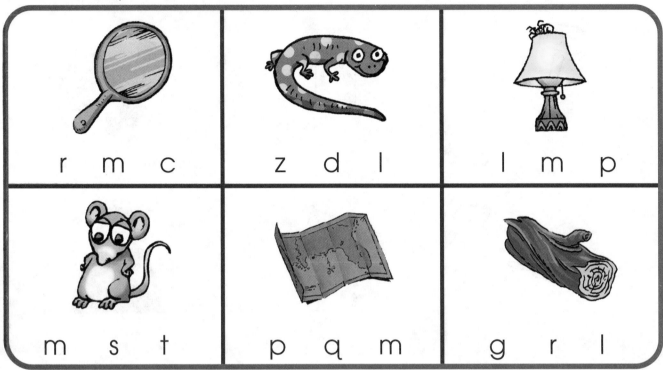

r   m   c   z   d   l   l   m   p

m   s   t   p   q   m   g   r   l

Directions: Say the name of each picture. Write the letter that shows the beginning sound of each picture name.

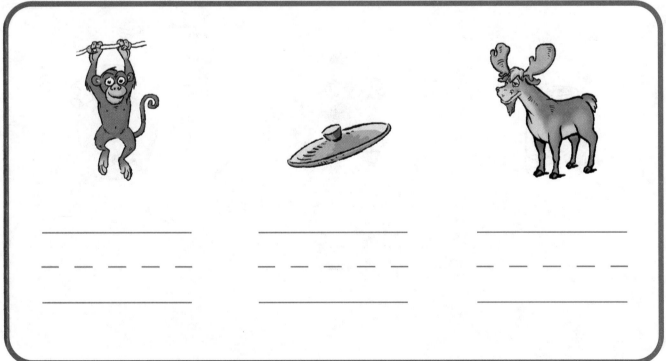

_____   _____   _____

_ _ _ _   _ _ _ _   _ _ _ _

_____   _____   _____

Consonants Review: N and P

Directions: Say the name of each picture. Circle the letter that shows the beginning sound of each picture name.

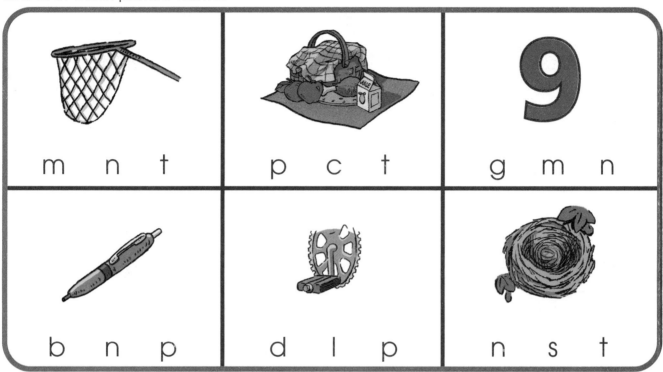

m n t	p c t	g m n
b n p	d l p	n s t

Directions: Say the name of each picture. Write the letter that shows the beginning sound of each picture name.

_____   _____   _____

- - - - - - - -   - - - - - - - -   - - - - - - - -

_____   _____   _____

Name _____

Consonants Review: Qu and R

Directions: Say the name of each picture. Circle the letter that shows the beginning sound of each picture name.

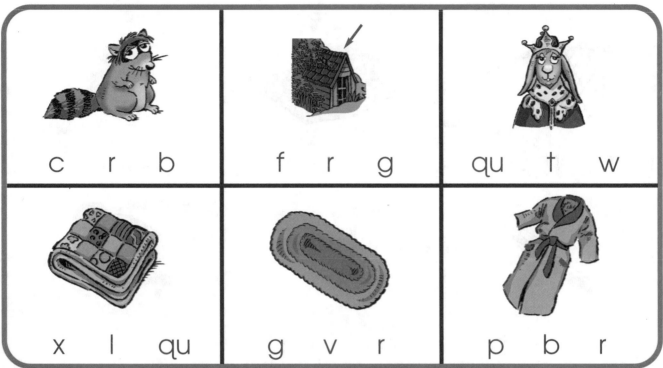

c   r   b   f   r   g   qu   t   w

x   l   qu   g   v   r   p   b   r

Directions: Say the name of each picture. Write the letter that shows the beginning sound of each picture name.

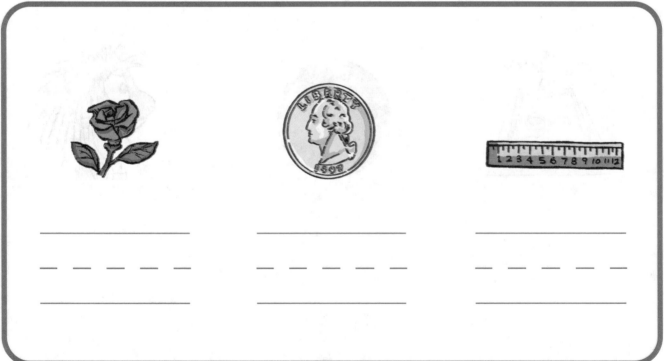

_____   _____   _____

Consonants Review: S and T

Directions: Say the name of each picture. Circle the letter that shows the beginning sound of each picture name.

s t p	b c t	p s c
t r l	s t w	w z s

Directions: Say the name of each picture. Write the letter that shows the beginning sound of each picture name.

_____

_____

_____

Consonants Review: V and W

Directions: Say the name of each picture. Circle the letter that shows the beginning sound of each picture name.

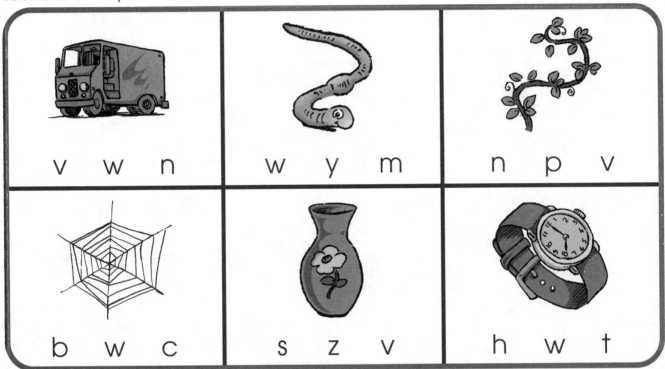

v   w   n   w   y   m   n   p   v

b   w   c   s   z   v   h   w   t

Directions: Say the name of each picture. Write the letter that shows the beginning sound of each picture name.

_____   _____   _____

_ _ _ _   _ _ _ _   _ _ _ _

_____   _____   _____

Consonants Review: Y and Z

Directions: Say the name of each picture. Circle the letter that shows the beginning sound of each picture name.

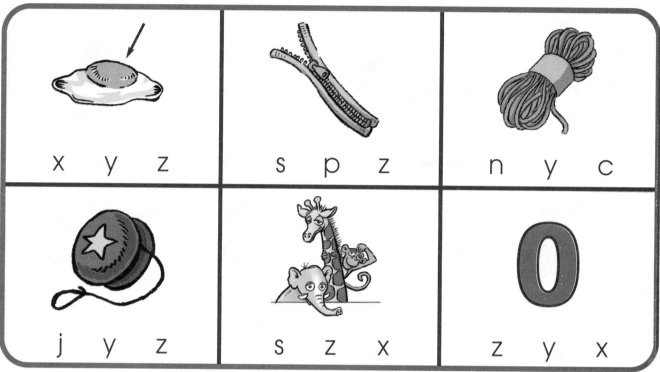

x y z   s p z   n y c

j y z   s z x   z y x

Directions: Say the name of each picture. Write the letter that shows the beginning sound of each picture.

_____   _____   _____

- - - - -   - - - - -   - - - - -

_____   _____   _____

Name _____

Review: Ending Sounds

Directions: Say the name of each picture. Circle the two pictures in each row whose names end with the same sound.

Review: Ending Sounds

Directions: Say the name of each picture. Circle the pictures in each row whose names have the same ending sound as the letter at the beginning of the row.

Review: Ending Sounds

Directions: Say the name of each picture. Circle the pictures in each row whose names have the same ending sound as the letter at the beginning of the row.

Name _____

Review: Ending Sounds

Directions: Say the name of each picture. Write the letter that shows the **ending** sound of each picture name.

Name _____

Consonants Review

Directions: Say the name of each picture. Write the missing letter of each picture name.

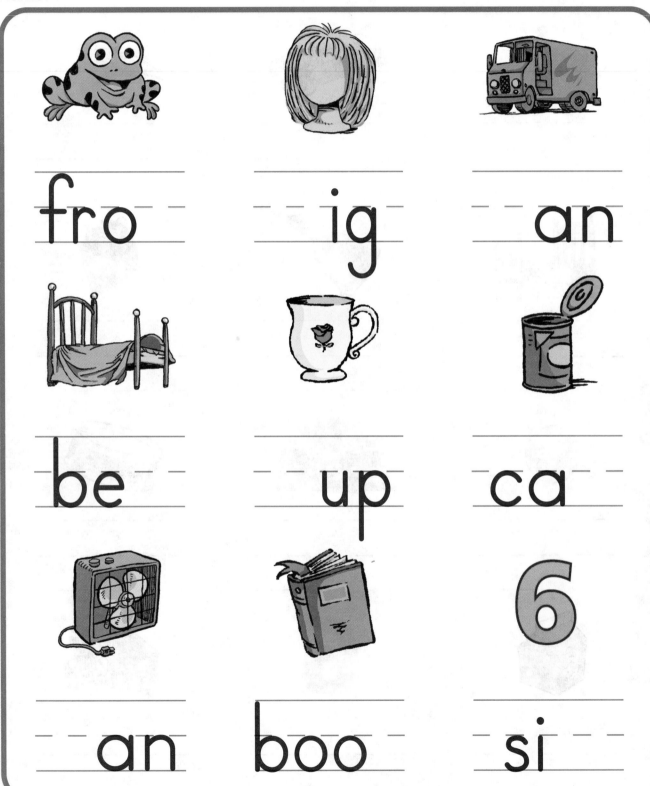

fro___

___ig

___an

be___

___up

ca___

___an

boo___

si___

Short a

Directions: Say the name of each picture. Draw an **X** through each picture whose name does **not** have the short **a** sound.

Short a

Directions: Say the name of each picture. Write the letter **a** below each picture whose name has the short **a** sound.

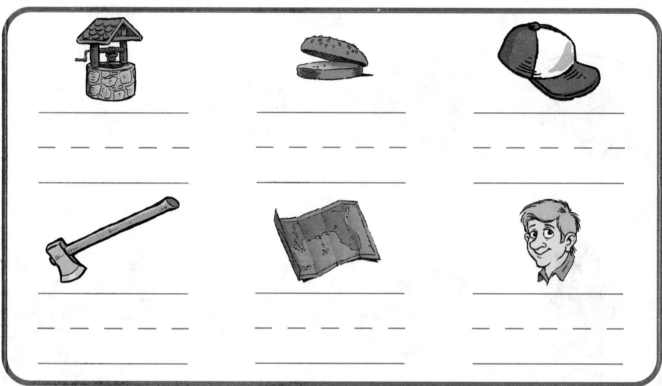

_____

Directions: Say the name of each picture. Write the letter **a** to complete each word.

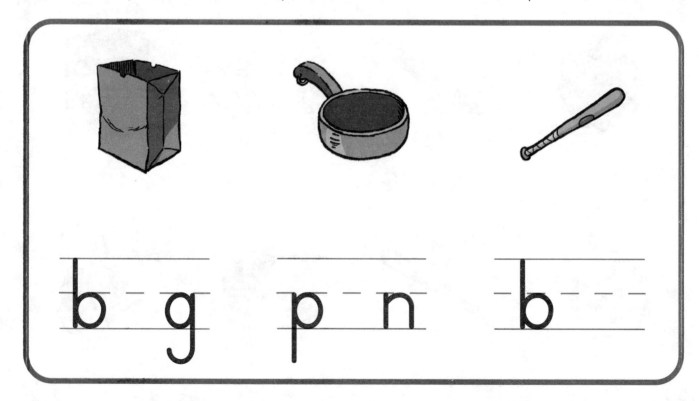

b g   p n   b

Name _____

Short a

Directions: Say the name of each picture. Draw a line to match each picture with its name.

van

bag

ant

pan

map

apple

tag

lamp

Short a

Directions: Say the name of each picture. Write the word from the Word Box that names each picture.

stamp	pan	can

_____

_ _ _ _ _ _ _

Directions: Write a word from the Word Box to complete each sentence.

hat	sat	man

_____

_ _ _ _ _ _ _

1. Little Critter _____ on the mat.

_____

_ _ _ _ _ _ _

2. That _____ is tall.

_____

_ _ _ _ _ _ _

3. I like my new _____.

Short e

Directions: Say the name of each picture. Draw an **X** through each picture that does **not** have the short **e** sound.

Short e

Directions: Say the name of each picture. Write the letter **e** below each picture that has the short **e** sound.

Directions: Say the name of each picture. Write the letter **e** to complete each word.

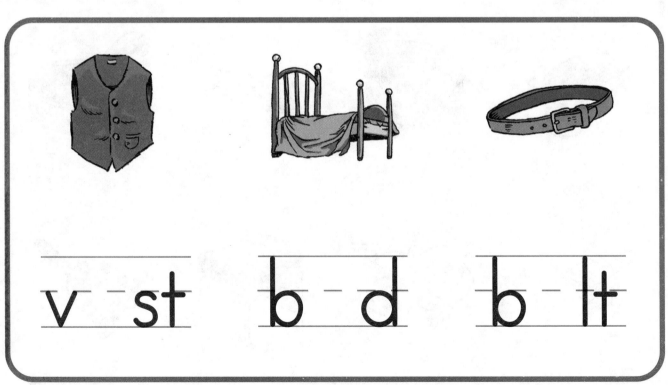

v ___ st   b ___ d   b ___ lt

Short e

Directions: Say the name of each picture. Draw a line to match each picture with its name.

desk

hen

bell

bed

sled

fence

check

steps

Short e

Directions: Say the name of each picture. Write the word from the Word Box that names each picture.

egg	net	jet

_____   _____   _____

- - - - - - -   - - - - - - -   - - - - - - -

_____   _____   _____

Directions: Write a word from the Word Box to complete each sentence.

bed	hen	beg

_____

- - - - - - -

1. The _____ sat on its nest.

   _____

   - - - - - - -

2. It is time for _____.

   _____

   - - - - - - -

3. My dog can _____.

Name _____

Review: Short a and Short e

Directions: Write the letter that shows the short vowel sound of each picture name.

Short i

Directions: Say the name of each picture. Draw an **X** through each picture that does **not** have the short **i** sound.

Short i

Directions: Say the name of each picture. Write the letter **i** below each picture that has the short **i** sound.

Directions: Say the name of each picture. Write the letter **i** to complete each word.

p __ g   l __ ps   l __ d

Short i

Directions: Say the name of each picture. Draw a line to match each picture with its name.

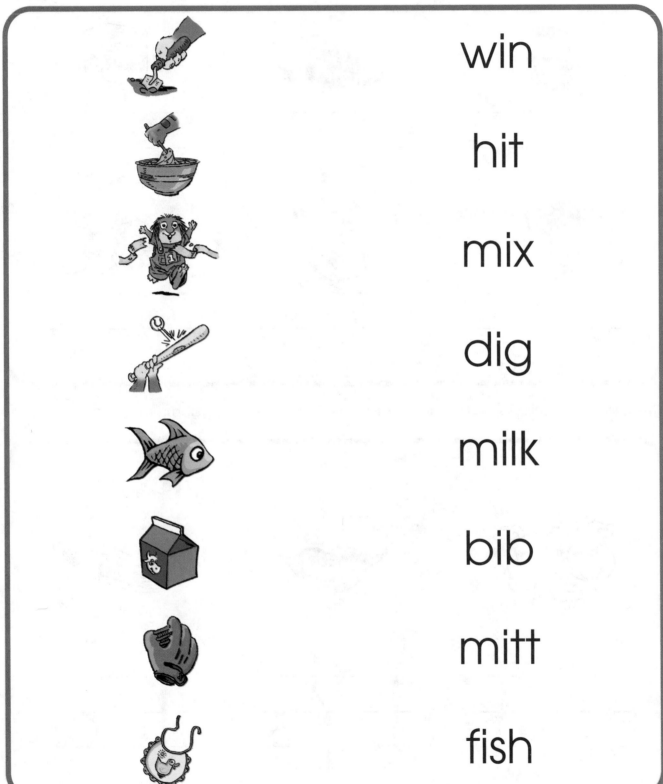

win

hit

mix

dig

milk

bib

mitt

fish

Short i

Directions: Say the name of each picture. Write the word from the Word Box that names each picture.

fish	lips	wig

_____   _____   _____

\- \- \- \- \-   \- \- \- \- \-   \- \- \- \- \-

_____   _____   _____

Directions: Write a word from the Word Box to complete each sentence.

hit	pig	lid

_____

\- \- \- \- \- \-

1. Put the _____ on the pan.

_____

\- \- \- \- \- \-

2. The _____ is in its pen.

_____

\- \- \- \- \- \-

3. Jim _____ the ball.

Short o

Directions: Say the name of each picture. Draw an **X** through each picture that does **not** have the short **o** sound.

Short o

Directions: Say the name of each picture. Write the letter **o** below each picture that has the short **o** sound.

Directions: Say the name of each picture. Write the letter **o** to complete each word.

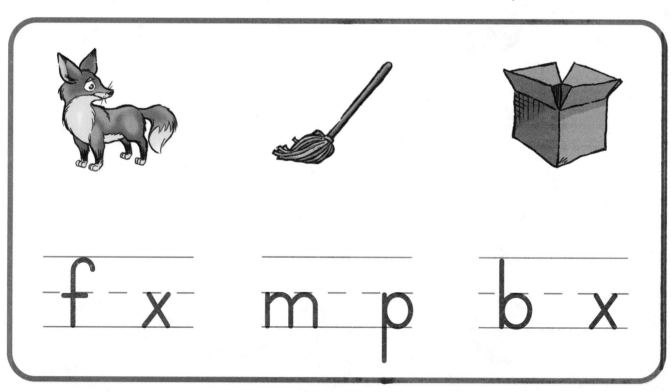

f ___ x   m ___ p   b ___ x

Short o

Directions: Say the name of each picture. Draw a line to match each picture with its name.

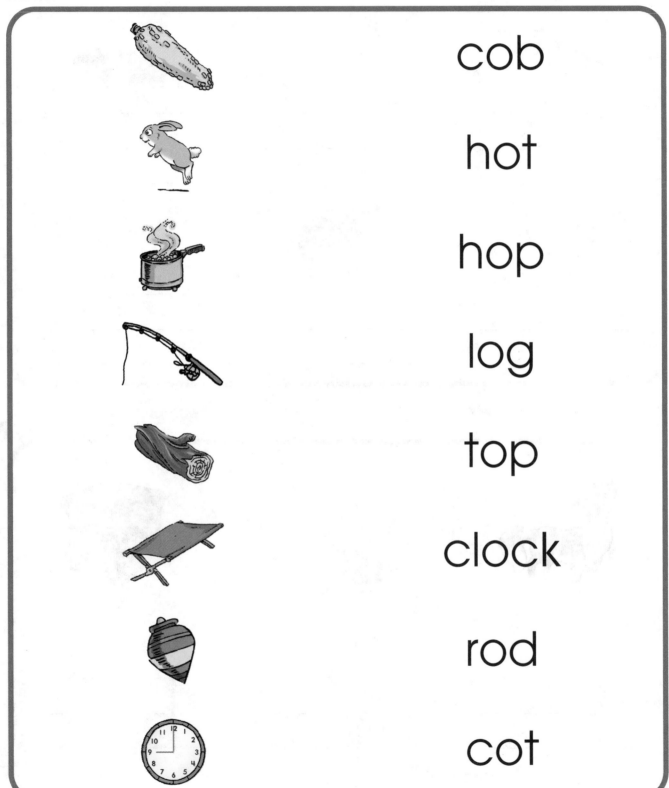

cob

hot

hop

log

top

clock

rod

cot

Short o

Directions: Say the name of each picture. Write the word from the Word Box that names each picture.

doll	hog	ox

_____

_ _ _ _ _ _ _

_____

Directions: Write a word from the Word Box to complete each sentence.

fox	hop	hot

_____

_ _ _ _ _ _

1. Watch the bunny _____.

_____

_ _ _ _ _ _

2. The pot is _____.

_____

_ _ _ _ _ _

3. See the red _____.

Review: Short i and Short o

Directions: Write the letter that shows the short vowel sound of each picture name.

Short u

Directions: Say the name of each picture. Draw an **X** through each picture that does **not** have the short **u** sound.

Name _____

Short u

Directions: Say the name of each picture. Write the letter **u** below each picture that has the short **u** sound.

Directions: Say the name of each picture. Write the letter **u** to complete each word.

h g   m   d   r

Name _____

Short u

Directions: Say the name of each picture. Draw a line to match each picture with its name.

mug

pup

bug

hug

sun

cup

bun

tub

Short u

Directions: Say the name of each picture. Write the word from the Word Box that names each picture.

rug	tub	sun

_____   _____   _____

_ _ _ _ _ _   _ _ _ _ _ _   _ _ _ _ _ _

_____   _____   _____

Directions: Write a word from the Word Box to complete each sentence.

bus	bun	hug

_____

_ _ _ _ _ _

1. I ride the _____.

_____

_ _ _ _ _ _

2. I _____ the baby.

_____

_ _ _ _ _ _

3. I ate the _____.

Review: Short Vowels

Directions: Say the name of each picture. Draw a line to match each picture with its name.

sock

tub

cat

hen

bug

well

hit

hop

Review: Short Vowels

Directions: Say the name of each picture. Write the letter that shows the short vowel sound of each picture name.

Directions: Say the name of each picture. Write the short vowel sound that completes each word.

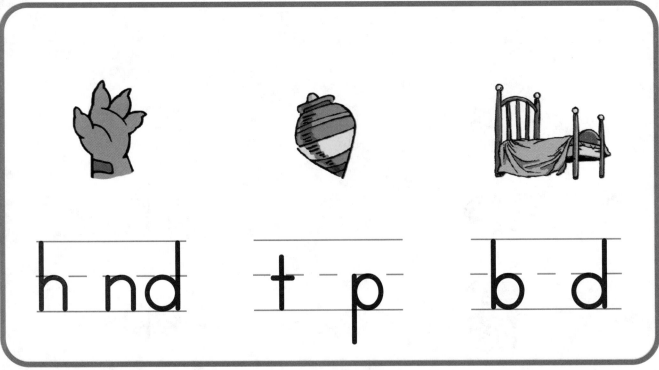

h _ n d   t _ p   b _ d

Review: Short Vowels

Directions: Say the name of each picture. Write the word from the Word Box that names each picture.

cot	bug	pan

_____   _____   _____

Directions: Write a word from the Word Box to complete each sentence.

fish	bat	sled

_____

1. I ride a _____.

2. The _____ is in the net.

3. Hit the ball with the _____.

Name _____

Review: Short Vowels

Directions: Draw a picture of something whose name has each short vowel sound.

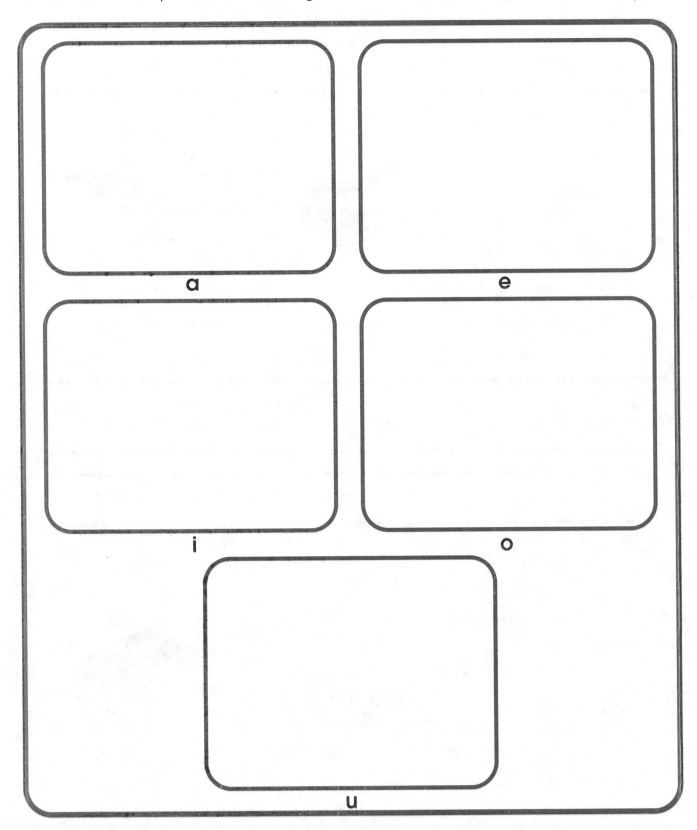

a

e

i

o

u

Name _____

Review: Short Vowels

Directions: Write the word from the Word Box that names each picture.

| man | mud | pig | egg | log | hen | ax | mix | pot |

Long a

Directions: Say the name of each picture. Color each picture whose name has the long **a** sound.

 g**a**m**e**

  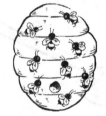

Name _____

Long a and Short a

Directions: Say the name of each picture. Draw a line to match each picture with its name.

wave

crab

cave

grapes

cap

ham

lamp

cane

Name _____

Long a

Directions: Write the word that rhymes with each long **a** word.

rake

_ _ _ _

cave

_ _ _ _

tape

_ _ _ _

mane

_ _ _ _

plate

_ _ _ _

Long a

Directions: Write a word from the Word Box to complete each sentence.

game	tape	vase	rake	cage	ape

1. Gabby put _____ on the present.

2. Mom set the _____ on the table.

3. We saw an _____ at the zoo.

4. The bird flew out of the _____.

5. Let's play a _____.

6. Dad gave me the _____.

Long i

Directions: Say the name of each picture. Color each picture whose name has the long **i** sound.

dim**e**

Long i and Short i

Directions: Say the name of each picture. Draw a line to match each picture with its name.

dime

dig

ride

six

fish

brick

dive

nine

Name ____________________

Long i

Directions: Write a word that rhymes with each long **i** word.

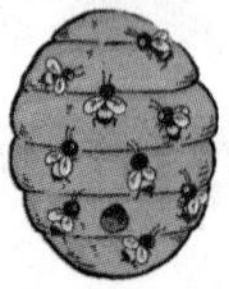

hive

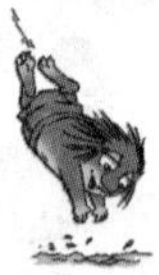

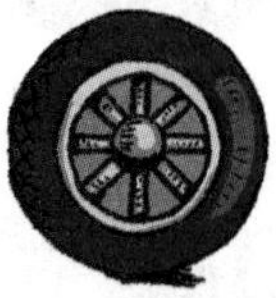

tire

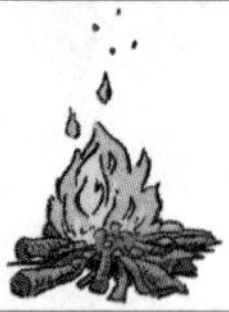

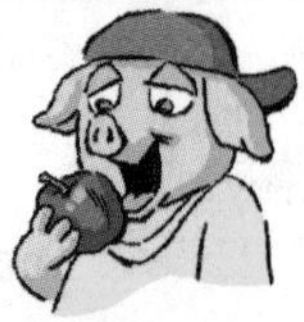

bite

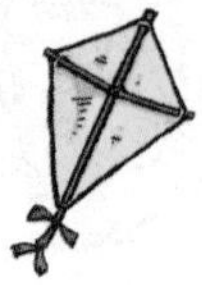

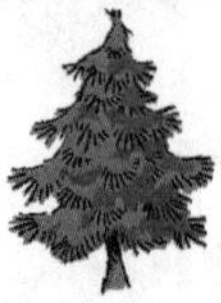

pine

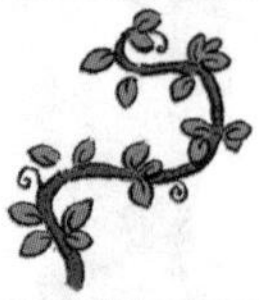

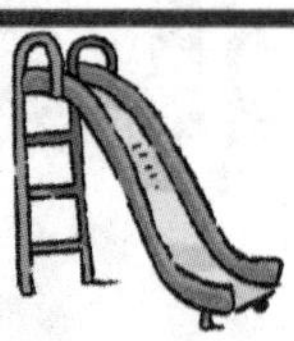

slide

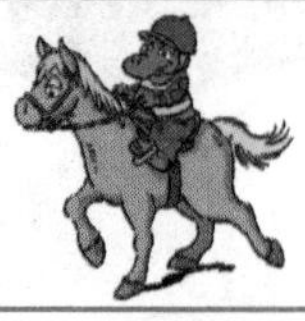

Long i

Directions: Write a word from the Word Box to complete each sentence.

| kite | nine | dive | bike | hive | bite |

1. I went down the slide _____ times.

2. Don't go near the bee's _____!

3. I like to ride my yellow _____.

4. Can you fly a _____?

5. Take a _____ of the apple.

6. I _____ into the water.

Review: Long a and Long i

Directions: Write the word from the Word Box that names each picture.

> cave pine wire tape rake pipes vase fire five

_____

- - - - - - - - - - - -

_____

_____

- - - - - - - - - - - -

_____

_____

- - - - - - - - - - - -

_____

_____

- - - - - - - - - - - -

_____

_____

- - - - - - - - - - - -

_____

_____

- - - - - - - - - - - -

_____

_____

- - - - - - - - - - - -

_____

_____

- - - - - - - - - - - -

_____

_____

- - - - - - - - - - - -

_____

Name _____

Long o

Directions: Say the name of each picture. Color each picture whose name has the long **o** sound.

nose

Long o and Short o

Directions: Say the name of each picture. Draw a line to match each picture with its name.

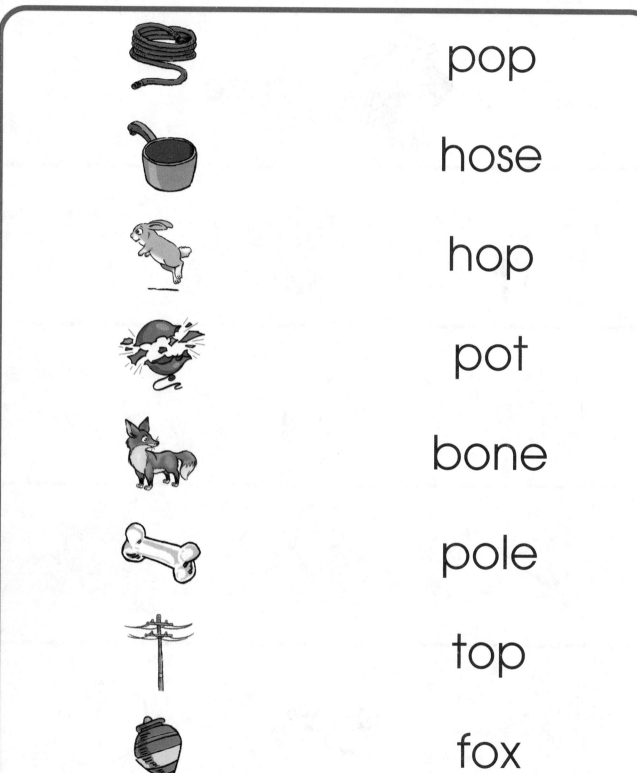

pop

hose

hop

pot

bone

pole

top

fox

Name _____

Long o

Directions: Write a word that rhymes with each long **o** word.

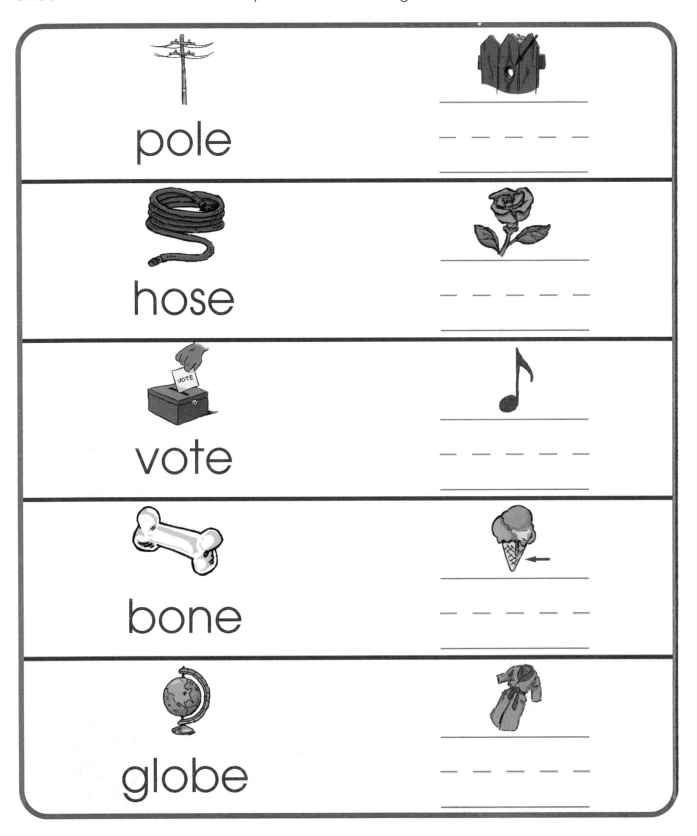

pole

hose

vote

bone

globe

Long o

Directions: Write a word from the Word Box to complete each sentence.

note	bone	nose	hose	rose	pole

1. Can you sing that _____?

2. Dad gave Mom a red _____.

3. Give the dog a _____.

4. I water the garden with the _____.

5. The bird sits on the _____.

6. The ball hit my _____.

Name _____

Long u

Directions: Say the name of each picture. Color each picture whose name has the long **u** sound.

 m**ule**

  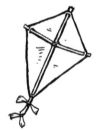

Long u and Short u

Directions: Say the name of each picture. Draw a line to match each picture with its name.

 bug

 mule

 tune

 tube

 tub

 cup

 mud

 rug

Long u

Directions: Say the name of each picture. Write the word from the Word Box that names each picture.

tube   ruler   cube   mule   tune   flute

_____

_ _ _ _ _ _ _ _

_____

_ _ _ _ _ _ _ _

_____

_ _ _ _ _ _ _ _

_____

_ _ _ _ _ _ _ _

_____

_ _ _ _ _ _ _ _

_____

_ _ _ _ _ _ _ _

Long u

Directions: Write a word from the Word Box to complete each sentence.

| ruler | mule | tube | cube | tune | flute |

1. Gabby saw a _____ at the farm.

2. Little Critter sings a _____.

3. Little Sister plays the _____.

4. Where is my _____?

5. I cannot find my _____ of glue.

6. I put a _____ of ice in my cup.

Review: Long o and Long u

Directions: Say the name of each picture. Write the word from the Word Box that names each picture.

mule   hose   tune   cube   cone   pole   tube   robe   note

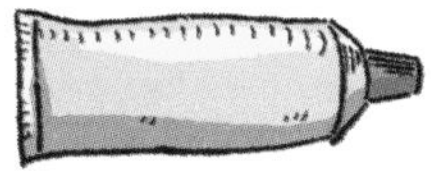

_____

_____

_____

_____

_____

_____

_____

_____

_____

Review: Long Vowels

Directions: Say the name of each picture. Write **a**, **i**, **o**, or **u** to show the vowel sound in each picture name.

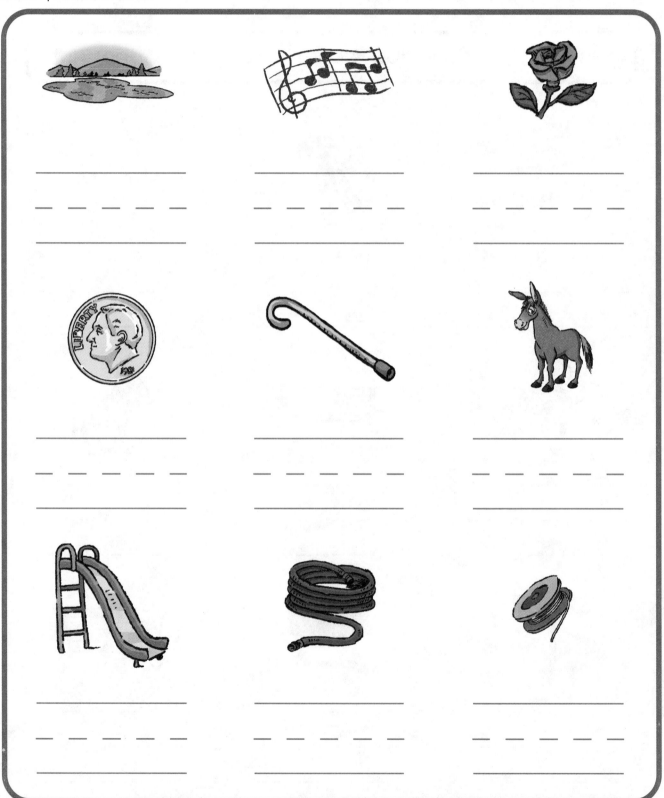

Review: Long Vowels

Directions: Say the name of each picture. Draw a line to match each picture with its name.

 cube

 cone

 tube

 bike

 tape

 mule

 rake

 five

Review: Long Vowels

Directions: Write the word from the Word Box that names each picture.

hole	nine	ride	tape	
game	dive	tune	robe	tube

_____   _____   _____

_____   _____   _____

_____   _____   _____

Review: Long Vowels

Directions: Write a word that rhymes with each word below.

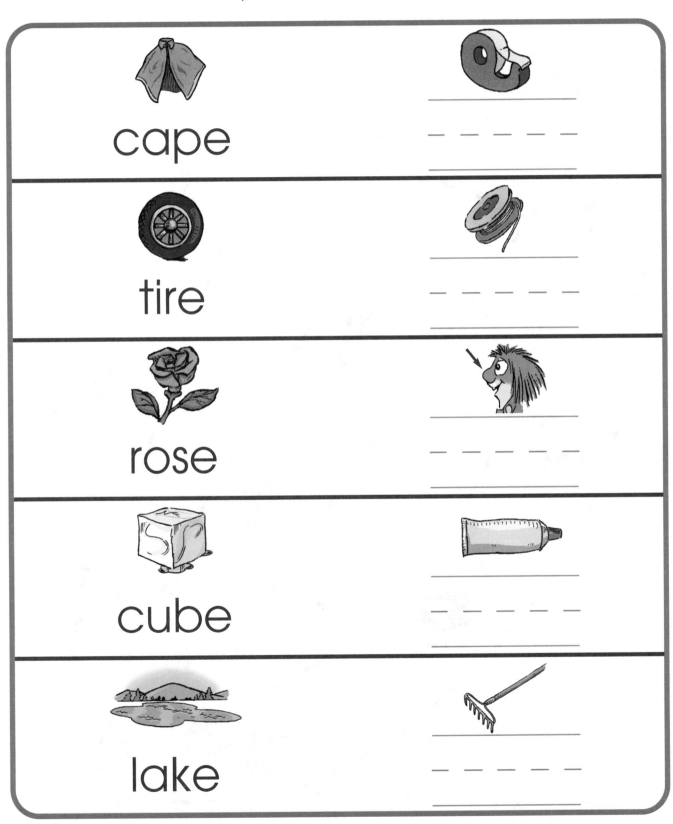

cape

tire

rose

cube

lake

Review: Long Vowels

Directions: Help Blue find his bone. Draw a line along the path of pictures whose names have long vowel sounds.

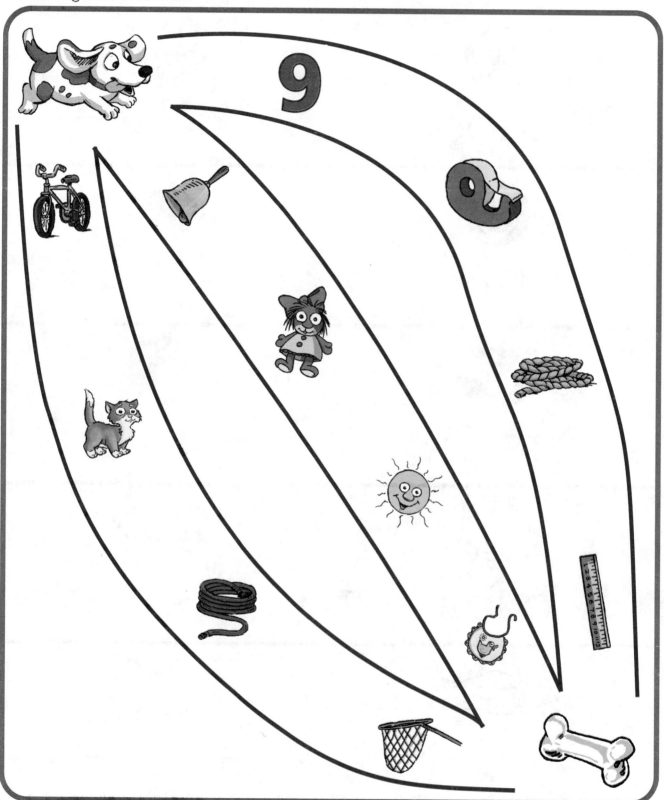

Review: Long Vowels

Directions: Write a word from the Word Box to complete each sentence.

tube	bike	kite	robe	game	rose

_____

_ _ _ _ _

1. The dog has a _____.

_____

_ _ _ _ _

2. Gator plays a _____.

_____

_ _ _ _ _

3. Little Sister wears a _____.

_____

_ _ _ _ _

4. The _____ is in the vase.

_____

_ _ _ _ _

5. Little Critter rides a _____.

_____

_ _ _ _ _

6. The _____ is on the bed.

Review: Long Vowels

Directions: Write a word from the Word Box to complete each sentence.

cape	bone	vine	tune	rope	mule

_____

— — — — — — — — —

1. Little Sister has on a _____.

_____

— — — — — — — — —

2. Little Critter rides a _____.

_____

— — — — — — — —

3. The _____ is on the bed.

_____

— — — — — — — —

4. Gator plays a _____.

_____

— — — — — — — —

5. The _____ is in the vase.

_____

— — — — — — — —

6. The dog has a _____.

Review: Long Vowels

Directions: Draw a picture of something whose name has each long vowel sound below.

A	
I	
O	
U	

Review: Long Vowels

Directions: Each picture name below has a long vowel sound. Write a sentence using each word.

_____	hive
_____	nose
_____	vase
_____	ruler

Review: Short and Long Vowels

Directions: Say the name of each picture. Draw a line to match each picture with its name.

 rose

 gate

 five

 bib

 tube

 fan

 hat

 belt

Review: Short and Long Vowels

Directions: Say the name of each picture. Write the word from the Word Box that names each picture below.

bun	dive	cave	desk	cob
cube	milk	man	home	

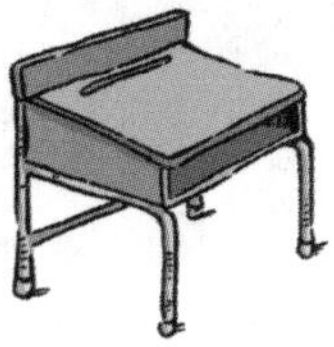

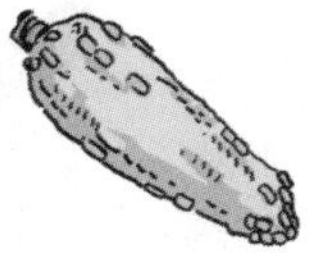

_____

_____

_____

_____

_____

_____

_____

_____

_____

_____

_____

_____

_____

_____

_____

_____

_____

_____

Review: Short and Long Vowels

Directions: Draw a picture of what each word names below.

jet	mane	nose
hop	bus	mule
pig	kite	bat

Review: Short and Long Vowels

Directions: Write a word or words from the Word Box to complete each sentence.

| cub | kit | bed | can | tube | cat | box | cape | tag |

1. The _____ is on the _____.

2. Dad has the _____.

3. Little Critter sees the _____.

4. I put the _____ in the _____.

5. The _____ plays with the _____.

6. Little Sister holds the _____.

Review: Short and Long Vowels

Directions: Write 6 words that have a **short** vowel sound.

Directions: Write 6 words that have a **long** vowel sound.

Directions: Write a sentence using two words from your lists above. Choose one word that has a **short** vowel sound and one word that has a **long** vowel sound.

Review: Short and Long Vowels

Directions: Write a word or words from the Word Box to complete each sentence.

cube cane kite box tape tub bed taps cap

1. Little Sister plays with the _____.

2. Dad has the _____.

3. Little Critter watches the _____.

4. The cat _____ the _____.

5. The _____ is on the _____.

6. She put the _____ in the _____.

Review: Short and Long Vowels

Directions: Make a new word by adding the letter **e** to each word below. Then, draw a picture to go with each new word. The first one is done for you.

cub — cube

pin _____

man _____

tub _____

can _____

Name _____

Consonant Blends With S

Directions: Say the name of each picture. Draw lines to match the pictures whose names have the same beginning blend.

82   Spectrum Phonics Grade 1

Name _____

Consonant Blends With S

Directions: Say the name of each picture. Circle the pictures in each row that have the same beginning blend.

Consonant Blends With S

Directions: Say the name of each picture. Write the **s** blend that completes each word.

sk	sl	sm	sp

___ ile

___ ate

___ ide

___ ip

___ in

___ ell

___ ed

___ ill

___ oon

Consonant Blends With S

Directions: Say the name of each picture. Write the **s** blend that completes each word.

sc	sn	st	sw

___ im

___ eps

___ ate

___ ap

___ arf

___ eep

___ amp

___ ow

___ ake

Review: Consonant Blends With S

Directions: Say the name of each picture. Write the word from the Word Box that names each picture.

| slide | spider | star | skate | |
| snail | steps | swan | smoke | scale |

_____
- - - - - - - - - - - - - - -
_____

_____
- - - - - - - - - - - - - - -
_____

_____
- - - - - - - - - - - - - - -
_____

_____
- - - - - - - - - - - - - - -
_____

_____
- - - - - - - - - - - - - - -
_____

_____
- - - - - - - - - - - - - - -
_____

Name _____

Consonant Blends With L

Directions: Say the name of each picture. Draw lines to match the pictures whose names have the same beginning blend.

Name _____

Consonant Blends With L

Directions: Say the name of each picture. Circle the pictures in each row whose names have the same beginning blend.

Consonant Blends With L

Directions: Say the name of each picture. Write the **l** blend that completes each word.

bl	cl	fl	gl	pl

_____ ade   _____ ate   _____ ap

_____ own   _____ ag   _____ obe

_____ ame   _____ ug   _____ ad

Consonant Blends With L

Directions: Draw a picture of what each word below names.

glass	plane	flag
plant	clam	flute
plate	flower	blanket

Name _____

Review: Consonant Blends With L

Directions: Say the name of each picture. Write the word from the Word Box that names each picture.

blow	clip	globe	flat	class
clock	glass	plane	plum	

_____
- - - - - - - - - - - - - - - - -
_____

_____
- - - - - - - - - - - - - - - - -
_____

_____
- - - - - - - - - - - - - - - - -
_____

Name _____

Consonant Blends With R

Directions: Say the name of each picture. Draw a line to match each picture whose name has the same beginning blend.

Name _____

Consonant Blends With R

Directions: Say the name of each picture. Circle the pictures in each row whose names have the same beginning blend.

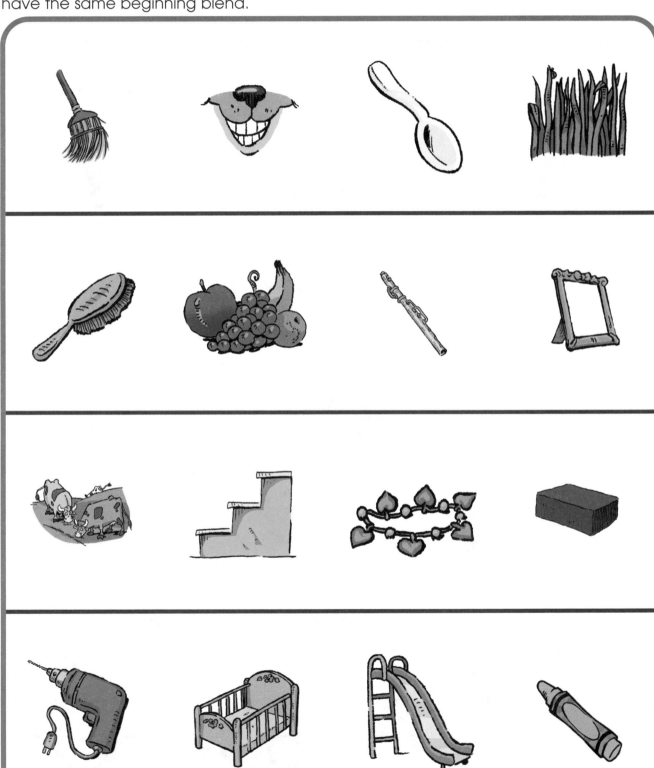

Consonant Blends With R

Directions: Say the name of each picture. Write the **r** blend that completes each word.

br	cr	dr	fr

_ _ _ og   _ _ _ ab   _ _ _ ill

_ _ _ ide   _ _ _ uit   _ _ _ ame

_ _ _ ip   _ _ _ ib   _ _ _ ead

Consonant Blends With R

Directions: Say the name of each picture. Write the **r** blend that completes each word.

gr	pr	tr

_____ ill   _____ apes   _____ ize

_____ ip   _____ ap   _____ in

_____ aze   _____ ain   _____ esent

Review: Consonant Blends With R

Directions: Say the name of each picture. Write the word from the Word Box that names each picture.

crayon	brush	dress	grass	truck
frame	prize	drum	broom	

_____   _____   _____

_____   _____   _____

_____   _____   _____

Name

Final Blends With S

Directions: Say the name of each picture. Circle the pictures in each row whose names have the same ending blend.

Final Blends With S

Directions: Say the name of each picture. Write the final **s** blend that completes each word.

sk	st

cru____   ve____   ca____

de____   li____   tu____

ma____   fi____   che____

Review: Final Blends With S

Directions: Say the name of each picture. Write the word from the Word Box that names each picture.

cast   tusk   desk   mask   nest   vest   fist   crust   list

_____ _____ _____

_____ _____ _____

_____ _____ _____

Name _____

Review: Consonant Blends

Directions: Say the name of each picture. Write the word from the Word Box that names each picture.

flag	smoke	plate	skirt	
broom	club	slide	grapes	stamp

_____   _____   _____

_____   _____   _____

_____   _____   _____

Name _____

Vowel Pairs: AI and AY

trai**n**   **h**ay

The vowel pairs **ai** and **ay** make the sound of long **a**.

Directions: Say the name of each picture. Draw a line to match each picture with its name.

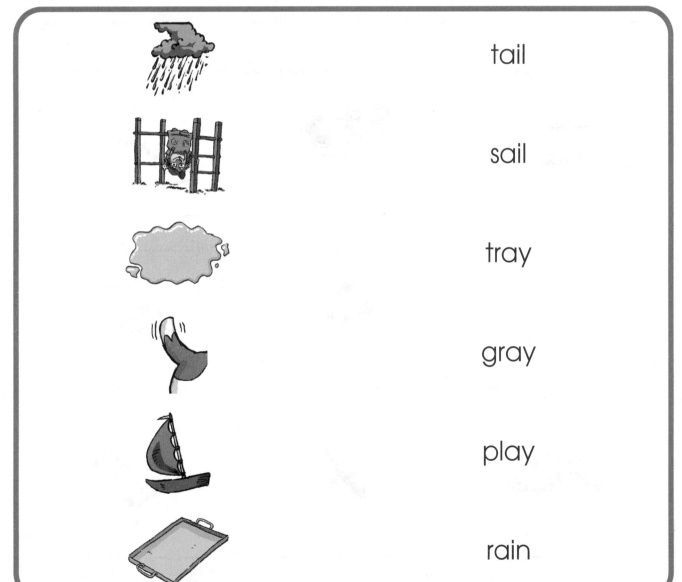

tail

sail

tray

gray

play

rain

Vowel Pairs: EE and EA

bee

bean

The vowel pairs **ee** and **ea** make the sound of long **e**.

Directions: Say the name of each picture. Write a word from the Word Box that names each picture.

meat   seat   feet   tea   leaf   heel   seal   beak   peas

_____ _____ _____

_____ _____ _____

_____ _____ _____

Name _____

Review: Vowel Pairs With A and E

Directions: Say the name of each picture. Write a word that rhymes with each word on the left.

pail

bee

train

hay

snail

Vowel Pairs: OA and OW

c**oa**t   wind**ow**

The vowel pairs **oa** and **ow** make the sound of long **o**.

Directions: Say the name of each picture. Draw a line to match each picture with its name.

   float

   goat

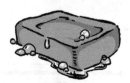   bowl

   snow

   soap

   crow

Name _____

Vowel Pair: OO

m**oo**n

The vowel pair **oo** makes the sound you hear in the middle of the word **moon**.

Directions: Write the missing letters **oo** for each word.

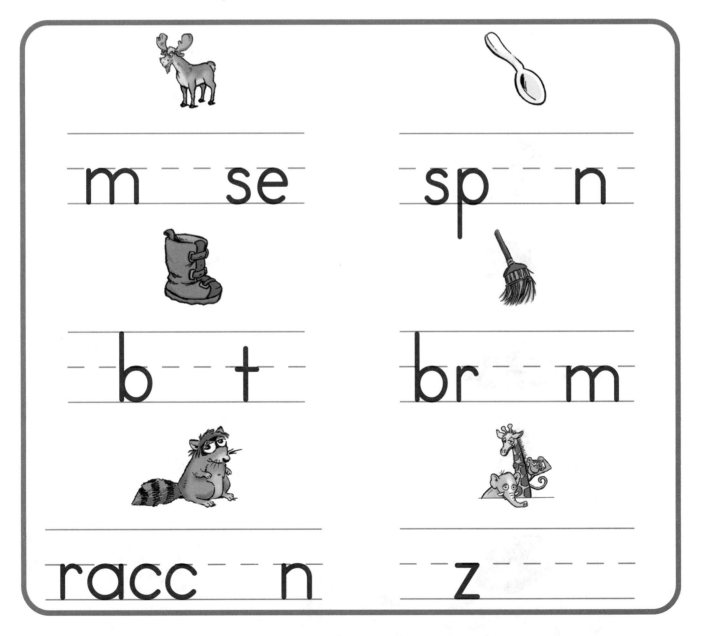

m__se   sp__n

b__t   br__m

racc__n   z__

Vowel Pair: OO

b**oo**k

The vowel pair **oo** makes another sound. It is the sound you hear in the middle of the word **book**.

Directions: Say the name of each picture. Draw a line to match each picture with its name.

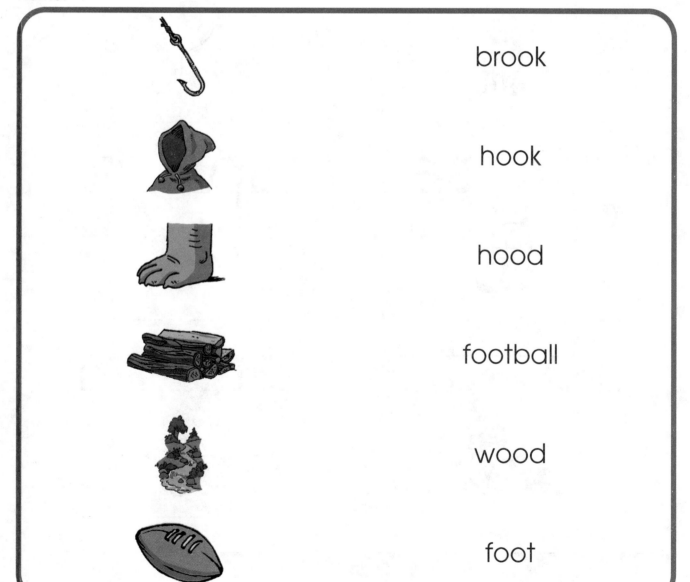

brook

hook

hood

football

wood

foot

Vowel Pair: OO

Directions: Each of the words below has the vowel pair **oo**. Draw a picture to go with each word.

foot	moose	hook
stool	pool	broom
tooth	boot	roof

Review: Vowel Pairs With OA, OO, OW

Directions: Say the name of each picture. Write the word from the Word Box that names each picture.

food	foot	woods	moon	
soap	pool	bowl	crow	toad

_____

_____

_____

_____

_____

_____

Y as Long i

fl**y**

In some words,
the letter **y** has
the long **i** sound.

Directions: Name each picture and write the word from the Word Box. Then, write two sentences. Use one word from the Word Box in each sentence.

cry	fry	fly	sky

1. _____

2. _____

Y as Long e

pony

In some words,
the letter **y** has
the long **e** sound.

Directions: Name each picture and write the word from the Word Box. Then, write two
sentences. Use one word from the Word Box in each sentence.

puppy	baby	lady	city

_____

_____

_____

_____

1. _____

_____

_____

2. _____

_____

_____

Review: The Sounds of Y

Directions: Each of the words below has one of the two sounds of **y**. Draw a picture of each word.

cry	pony	penny
sky	baby	lady
fly	bunny	fry

Review: Vowel Pairs and Sounds of Y

Directions: Say the name of each picture. Write the word from the Word Box that names each picture.

rain	float	book	puppy	
hood	feet	row	leaf	hay

Consonant Pairs: CH and SH

Examples:

chair   **sh**oe

Directions: Say the name of each picture. Circle the pictures in each row that have the same beginning sound.

Consonant Pairs: CH and SH

Directions: Say the name of each picture. Draw lines to match each picture with its name.

 sheep

 shed

 chin

 shave

 chop

 shell

 cheek

 chain

Consonant Pairs: TH and WH

Examples:

thin   **wh**eel

Directions: Say the name of each picture. Write the letters **th** or **wh** to complete each word.

_____ istle   _____ isker

_____ orn   _____ ree

_____ read   _____ ale

Consonant Pairs: TH and WH

Directions: Name each picture and write the word from the Word Box. Then, write two sentences. Use one word from the Word Box in each sentence.

wheelchair	whale	whisker
thorn	wheel	thirteen

1. _____

2. _____

Consonant Pairs Endings: CH, SH, TH

Examples: ea**ch**   wi**sh**   wi**th**

Directions: Say the name of each picture. Circle the pictures that have the same ending sounds.

Consonant Pairs Endings: CH, SH, TH

Examples: ea**ch** wi**sh** wi**th**

Directions: Name each picture and circle the consonant pair that shows the ending sound. Then, write two sentences. Use one word from above in each sentence.

ch sh th	ch sh th	ch sh th
ch sh th	ch sh th	ch sh th
ch sh th	ch sh th	ch sh th

1. _____

_____

2. _____

Consonant Pair: NG

Example:

ri**ng**

Directions: Write the consonant pair **ng** below each picture whose name ends with the sound of **ng**.

Consonant Pair: NG

Directions: Say the name of each picture. Draw lines to match each picture with its name.

king

sing

hang

wing

string

swing

ring

song

Review: Consonant Pairs

Directions: Say each word. Draw a picture of each word.

chain	thorn	swing
sheep	fish	bath
wheel	bench	chest

Review: Consonant Pairs

Directions: Say the name of each picture. Write a word from the Word Box that names each picture.

wing	thirteen	swing	tooth	bench
wheel	brush	bath	song	

_____

_____

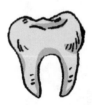

_____

_____

_____

_____

_____

_____

_____

Letters and Their Sounds

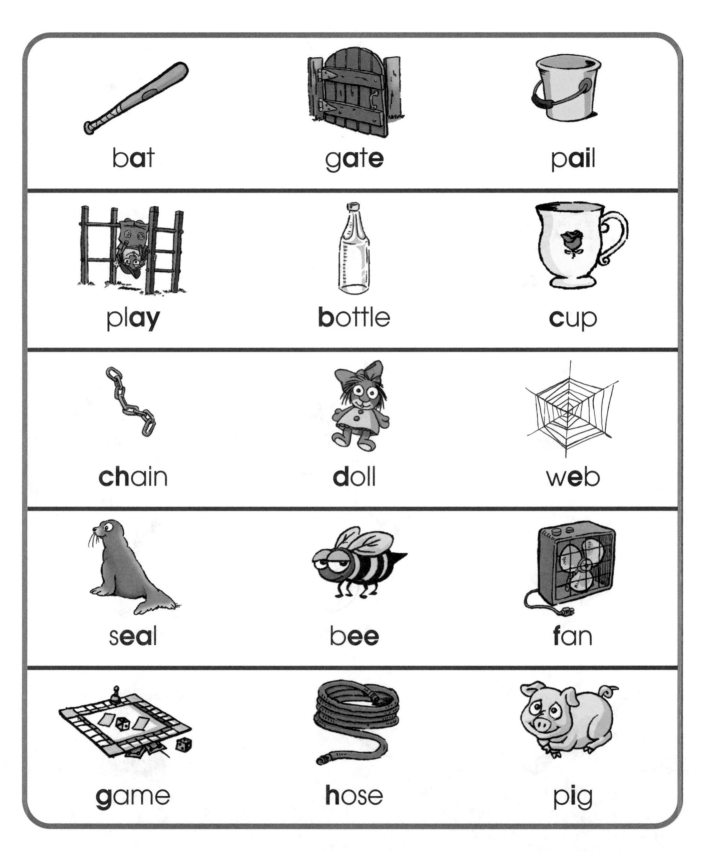

b**a**t

g**ate**

p**ai**l

p**lay**

bottle

cup

chain

doll

w**e**b

s**ea**l

b**ee**

fan

game

hose

p**i**g

Letters and Their Sounds

dime

jar

kangaroo

lizard

monkey

nine

king

fox

soap

rose

spoon

hook

crow

pen

queen

Letters and Their Sounds

radio   **s**aw   **sh**ip

turtle   **th**umb   r**u**g

mule   **v**an   **w**ell

whale   a**x**   **y**arn

sk**y**   pupp**y**   **z**ipper

Practice Page

Practice Page

Practice Page

Answer Key

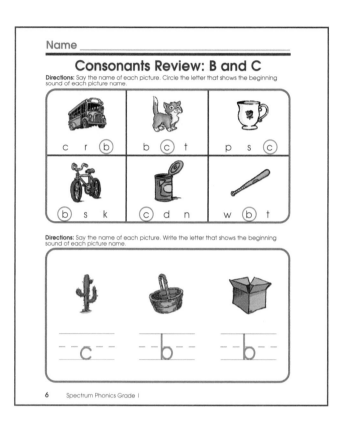

Consonants Review: B and C

Directions: Say the name of each picture. Circle the letter that shows the beginning sound of each picture name.

c   r   (b)   b   (c)   t   p   s   (c)

(b)   s   k   (c)   d   n   w   (b)   t

Directions: Say the name of each picture. Write the letter that shows the beginning sound of each picture name.

c   b   b

Consonants Review: D and F

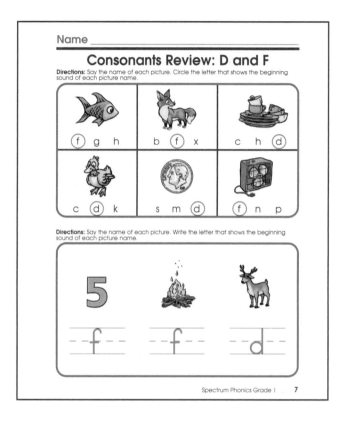

Directions: Say the name of each picture. Circle the letter that shows the beginning sound of each picture name.

(f)   g   h   b   (f)   x   c   h   (d)

c   (d)   k   s   m   (d)   (f)   n   p

Directions: Say the name of each picture. Write the letter that shows the beginning sound of each picture name.

f   f   d

Consonants Review: G and H

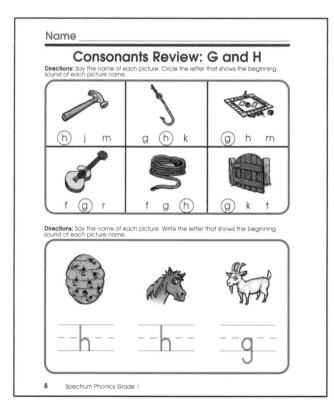

Directions: Say the name of each picture. Circle the letter that shows the beginning sound of each picture name.

(h)   j   m   g   (h)   k   (g)   h   m

f   (g)   r   f   g   (h)   (g)   k   t

Directions: Say the name of each picture. Write the letter that shows the beginning sound of each picture name.

h   h   g

Consonants Review: J and K

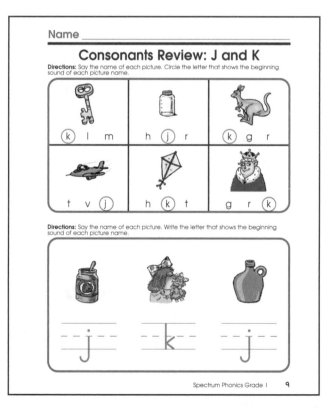

Directions: Say the name of each picture. Circle the letter that shows the beginning sound of each picture name.

(k)   l   m   h   (j)   r   (k)   g   r

t   v   (j)   h   (k)   t   g   r   (k)

Directions: Say the name of each picture. Write the letter that shows the beginning sound of each picture name.

j   k   j

Answer Key

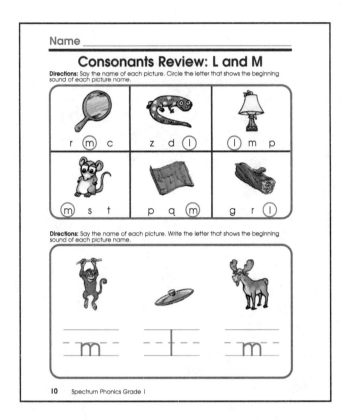

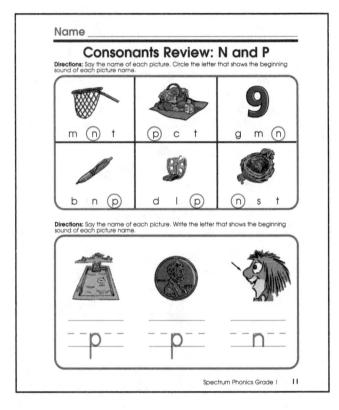

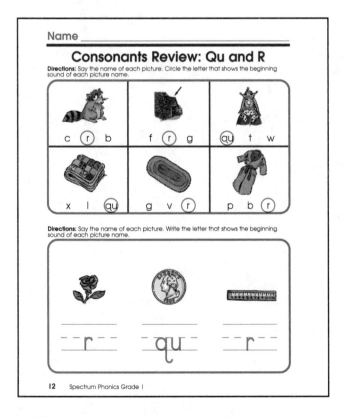

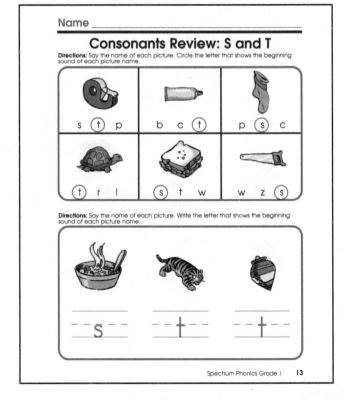

Answer Key

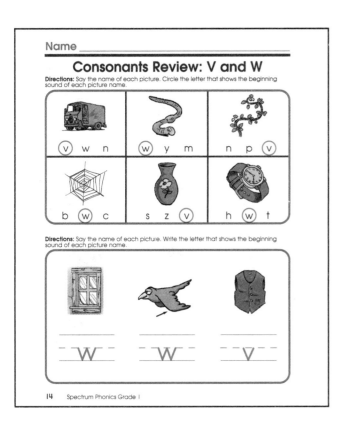

Consonants Review: V and W

Directions: Say the name of each picture. Circle the letter that shows the beginning sound of each picture name.

(v) w n   (w) y m   n p (v)

b (w) c   s z (v)   h (w) t

Directions: Say the name of each picture. Write the letter that shows the beginning sound of each picture name.

W   W   V

14   Spectrum Phonics Grade 1

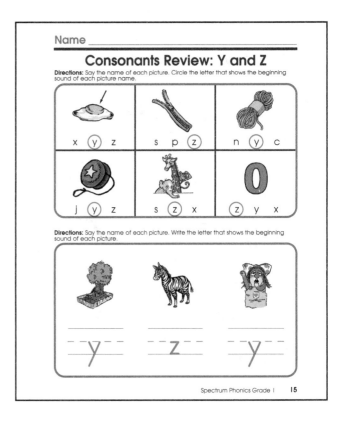

Consonants Review: Y and Z

Directions: Say the name of each picture. Circle the letter that shows the beginning sound of each picture name.

x (y) z   s p (z)   n (y) c

j (y) z   s (z) x   (z) y x

Directions: Say the name of each picture. Write the letter that shows the beginning sound of each picture.

y   z   y

Spectrum Phonics Grade 1   15

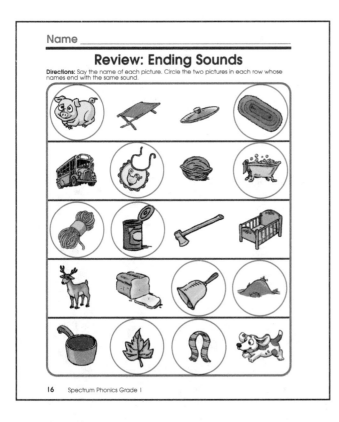

Review: Ending Sounds

Directions: Say the name of each picture. Circle the two pictures in each row whose names end with the same sound.

16   Spectrum Phonics Grade 1

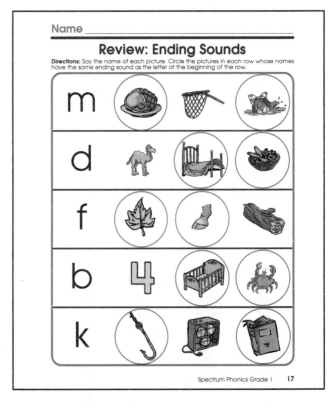

Review: Ending Sounds

Directions: Say the name of each picture. Circle the pictures in each row whose names have the same ending sound as the letter at the beginning of the row.

m

d

f

b

k

Spectrum Phonics Grade 1   17

Answer Key

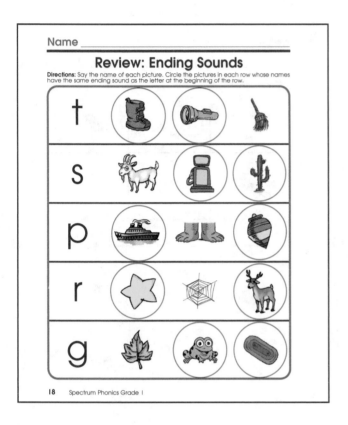

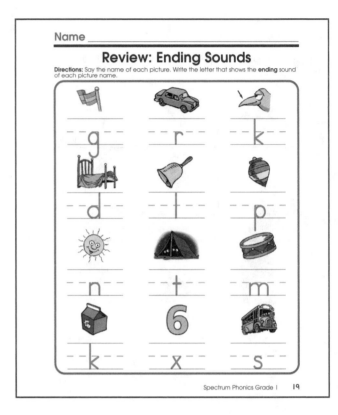

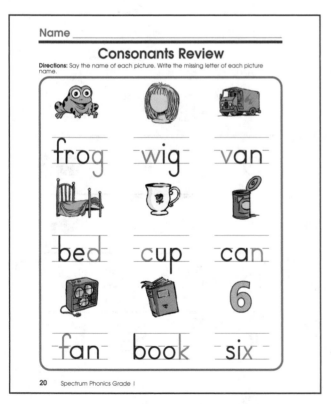

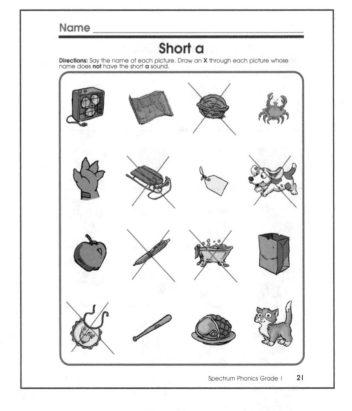

Answer Key

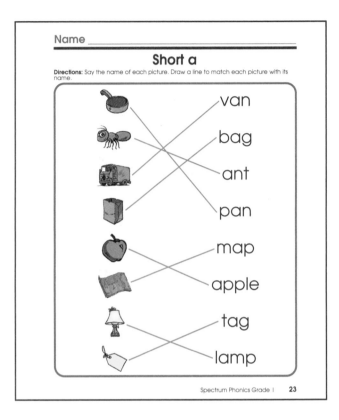

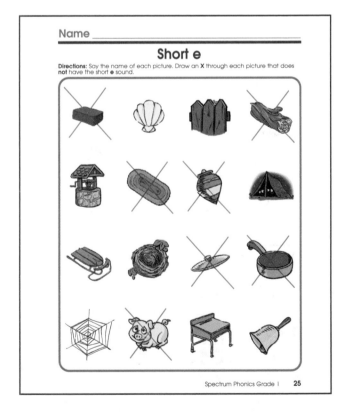

Answer Key

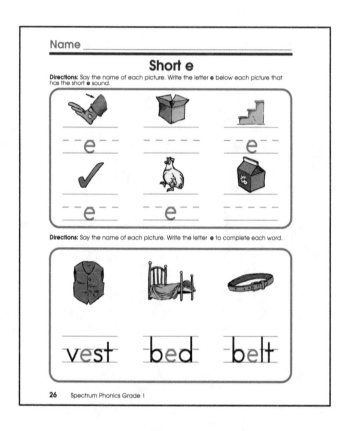

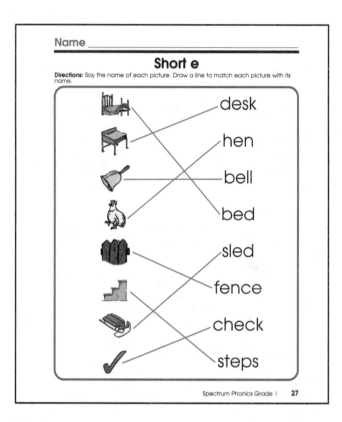

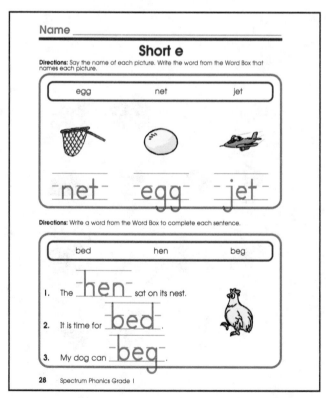

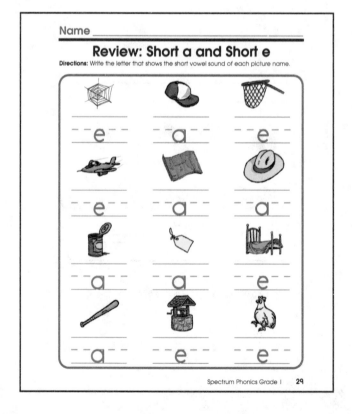

Answer Key

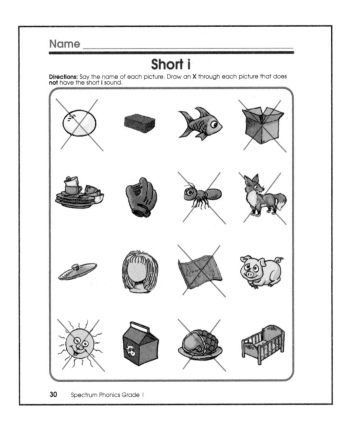

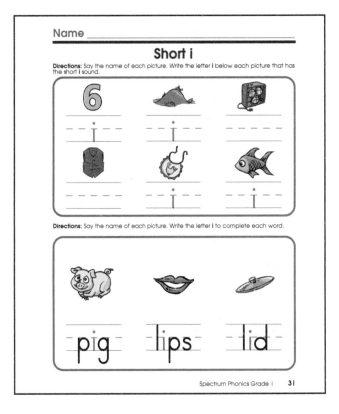

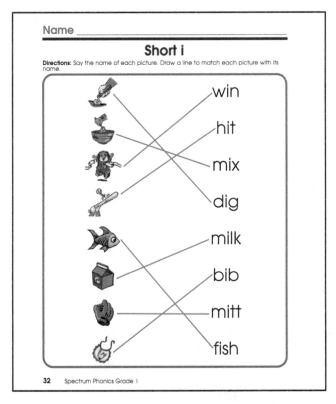

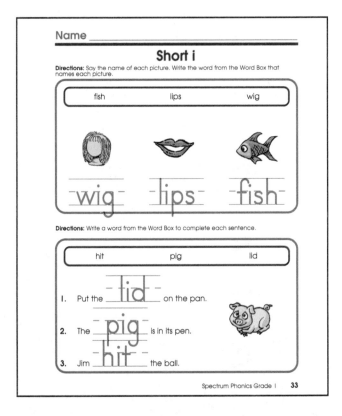

Answer Key

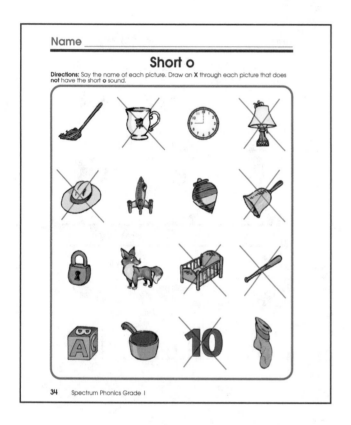

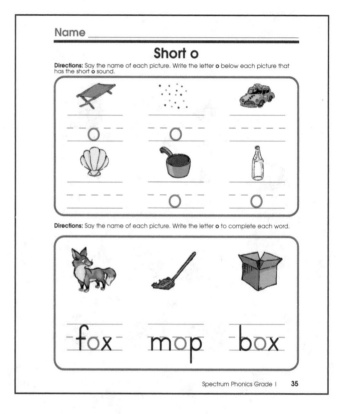

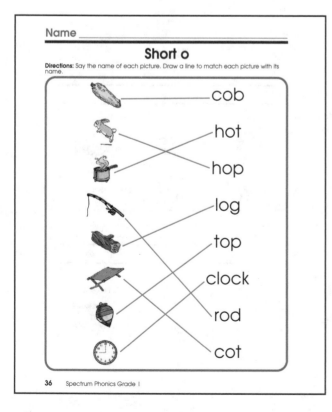

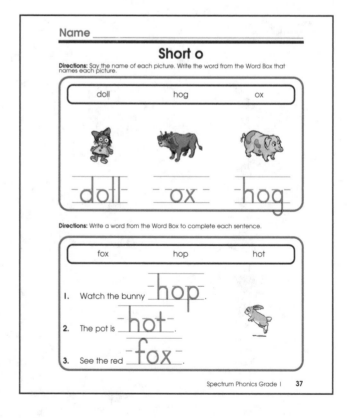

Answer Key

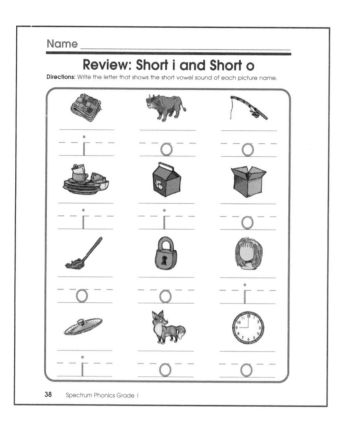

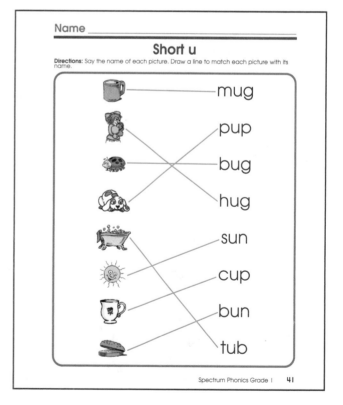

Answer Key

Name

Short u

Directions: Say the name of each picture. Write the word from the Word Box that names each picture.

rug	tub	sun

sun rug tub

Directions: Write a word from the Word Box to complete each sentence.

bus	bun	hug

1. I ride the bus
2. I hug the baby.
3. I ate the bun.

42 Spectrum Phonics Grade 1

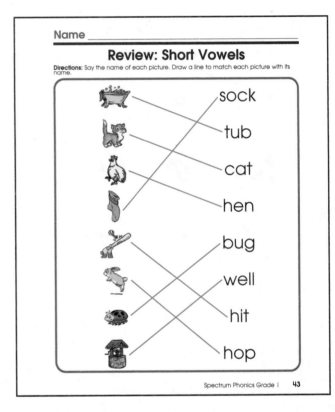

Name

Review: Short Vowels

Directions: Say the name of each picture. Draw a line to match each picture with its name.

- sock
- tub
- cat
- hen
- bug
- well
- hit
- hop

Spectrum Phonics Grade 1   43

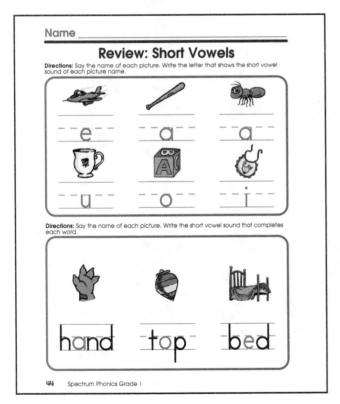

Name

Review: Short Vowels

Directions: Say the name of each picture. Write the letter that shows the short vowel sound of each picture name.

e   a   a
u   o   i

Directions: Say the name of each picture. Write the short vowel sound that completes each word.

hand   top   bed

44 Spectrum Phonics Grade 1

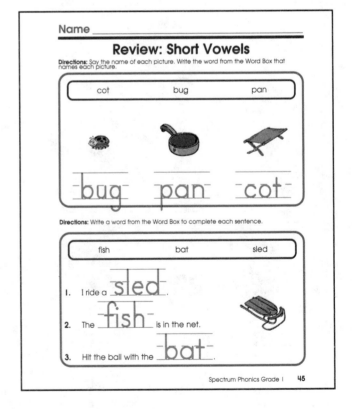

Name

Review: Short Vowels

Directions: Say the name of each picture. Write the word from the Word Box that names each picture.

cot	bug	pan

bug pan cot

Directions: Write a word from the Word Box to complete each sentence.

fish	bat	sled

1. I ride a sled.
2. The fish is in the net.
3. Hit the ball with the bat.

Spectrum Phonics Grade 1   45

138   Spectrum Phonics Grade 1

Answer Key

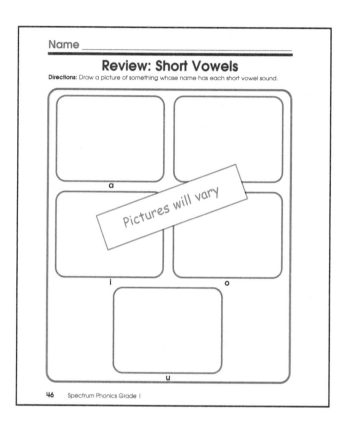

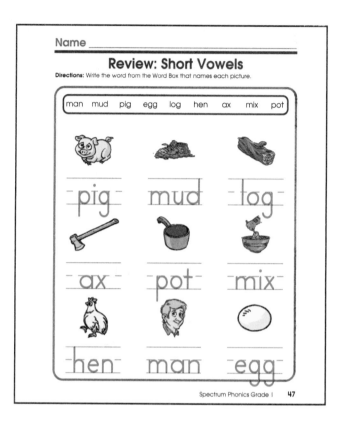

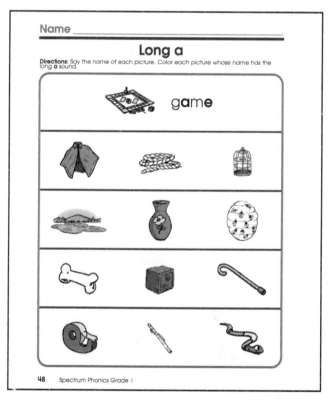

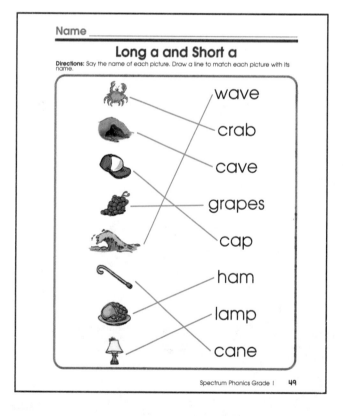

Answer Key

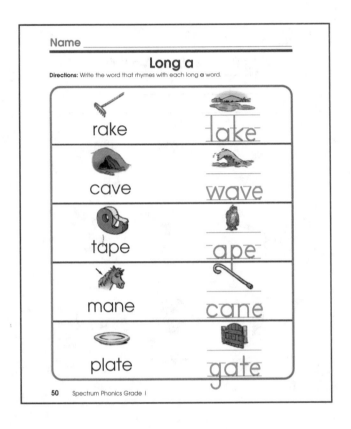

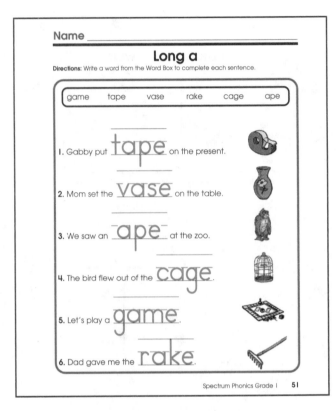

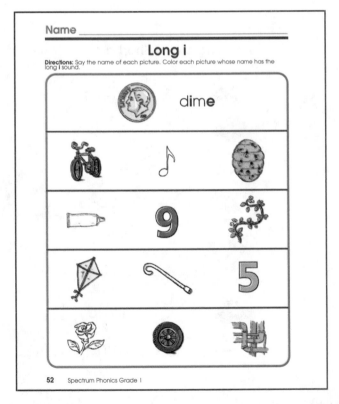

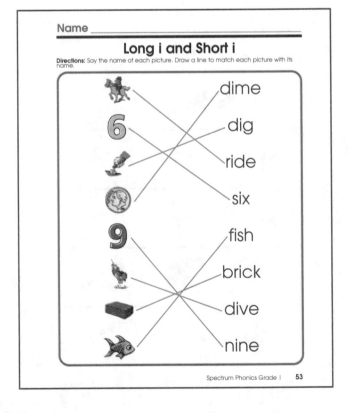

Answer Key

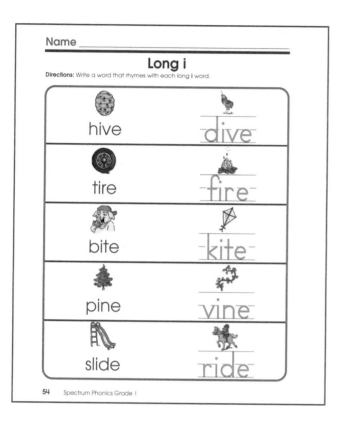

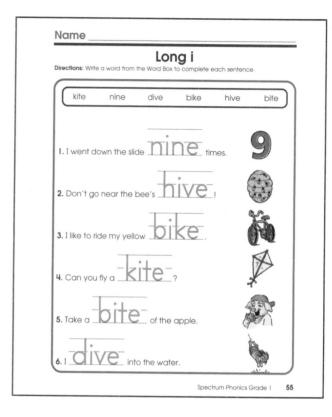

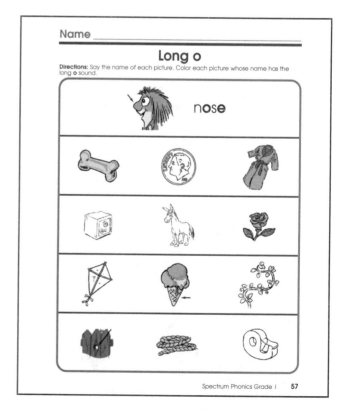

Answer Key

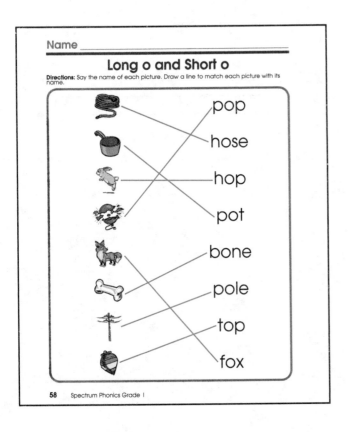

Name _____

Long o and Short o

Directions: Say the name of each picture. Draw a line to match each picture with its name.

pop

hose

hop

pot

bone

pole

top

fox

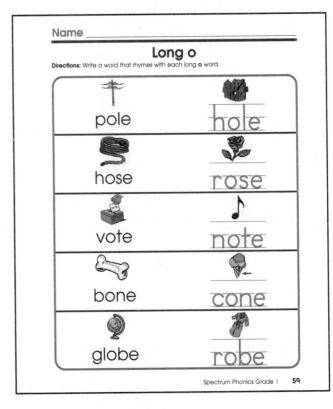

Name _____

Long o

Directions: Write a word that rhymes with each long **o** word.

pole	hole
hose	rose
vote	note
bone	cone
globe	robe

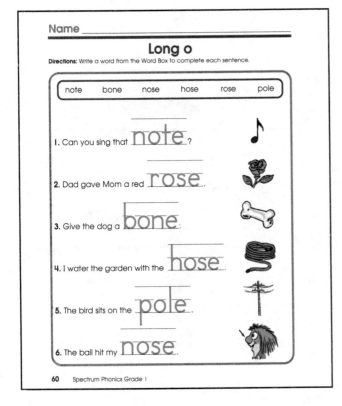

Name _____

Long o

Directions: Write a word from the Word Box to complete each sentence.

| note | bone | nose | hose | rose | pole |

1. Can you sing that note?

2. Dad gave Mom a red rose

3. Give the dog a bone.

4. I water the garden with the hose

5. The bird sits on the pole

6. The ball hit my nose.

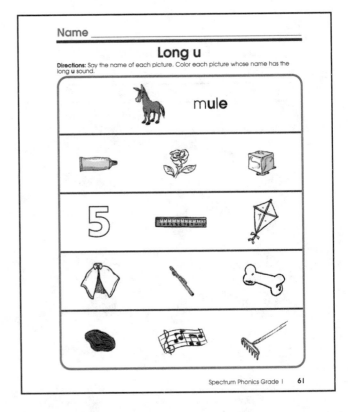

Name _____

Long u

Directions: Say the name of each picture. Color each picture whose name has the long **u** sound.

mule

5

Answer Key

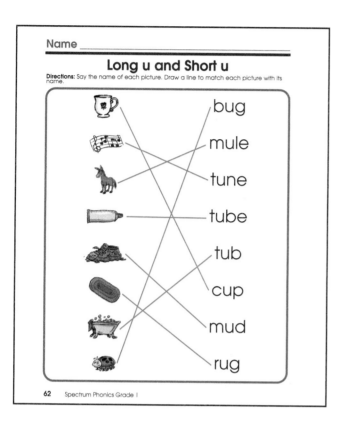

Name _____

Long u and Short u

Directions: Say the name of each picture. Draw a line to match each picture with its name.

bug

mule

tune

tube

tub

cup

mud

rug

62   Spectrum Phonics Grade 1

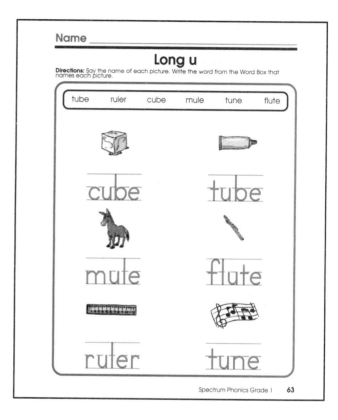

Name _____

Long u

Directions: Say the name of each picture. Write the word from the Word Box that names each picture.

| tube | ruler | cube | mule | tune | flute |

cube   tube

mute   flute

ruler   tune

Spectrum Phonics Grade 1   63

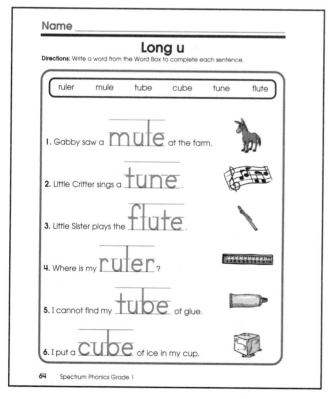

Name _____

Long u

Directions: Write a word from the Word Box to complete each sentence.

| ruler | mule | tube | cube | tune | flute |

1. Gabby saw a mule at the farm.

2. Little Critter sings a tune.

3. Little Sister plays the flute.

4. Where is my ruler?

5. I cannot find my tube of glue.

6. I put a cube of ice in my cup.

64   Spectrum Phonics Grade 1

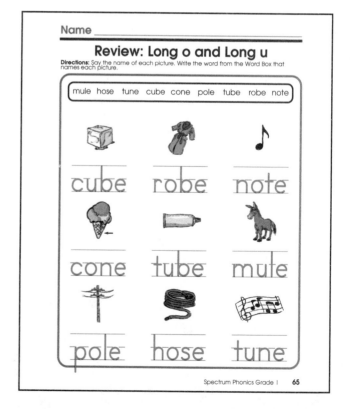

Name _____

Review: Long o and Long u

Directions: Say the name of each picture. Write the word from the Word Box that names each picture.

| mule | hose | tune | cube | cone | pole | tube | robe | note |

cube   robe   note

cone   tube   mute

pole   hose   tune

Spectrum Phonics Grade 1   65

Answer Key

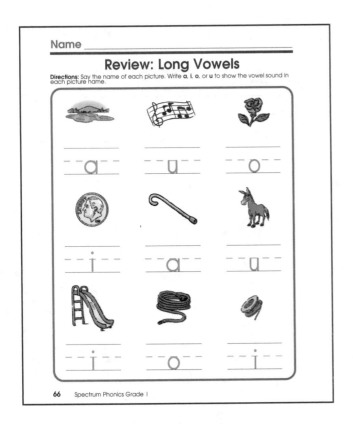

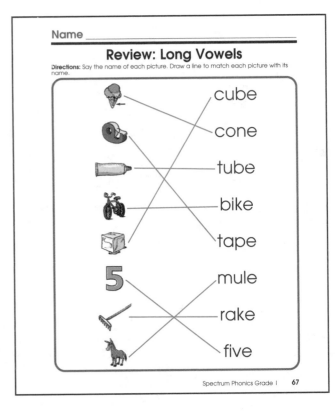

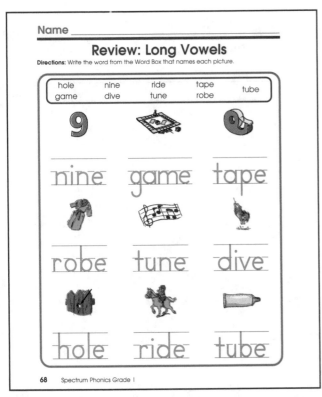

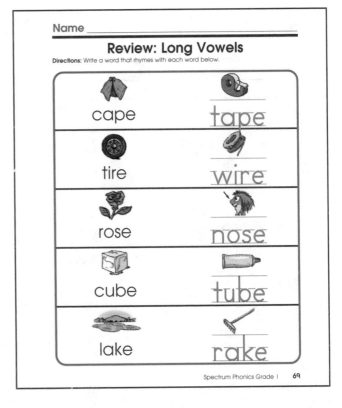

Answer Key

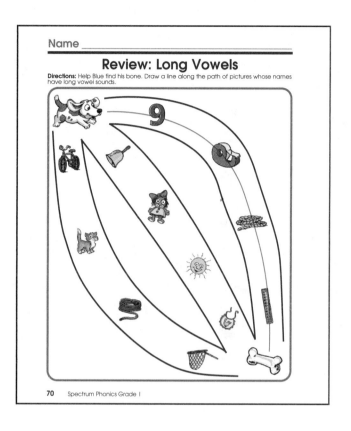

Name _____

Review: Long Vowels

Directions: Help Blue find his bone. Draw a line along the path of pictures whose names have long vowel sounds.

70   Spectrum Phonics Grade 1

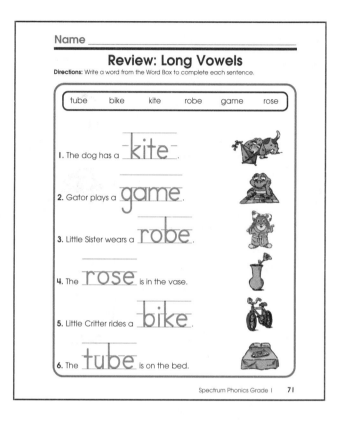

Name _____

Review: Long Vowels

Directions: Write a word from the Word Box to complete each sentence.

tube	bike	kite	robe	game	rose

1. The dog has a __kite__.

2. Gator plays a __game__.

3. Little Sister wears a __robe__.

4. The __rose__ is in the vase.

5. Little Critter rides a __bike__.

6. The __tube__ is on the bed.

Spectrum Phonics Grade 1   71

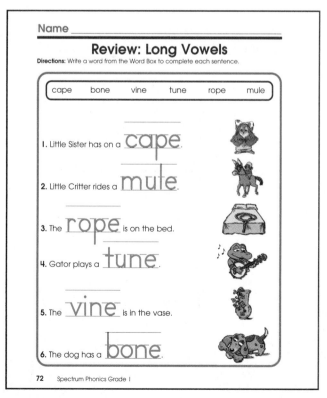

Name _____

Review: Long Vowels

Directions: Write a word from the Word Box to complete each sentence.

cape	bone	vine	tune	rope	mule

1. Little Sister has on a __cape__.

2. Little Critter rides a __mule__.

3. The __rope__ is on the bed.

4. Gator plays a __tune__.

5. The __vine__ is in the vase.

6. The dog has a __bone__.

72   Spectrum Phonics Grade 1

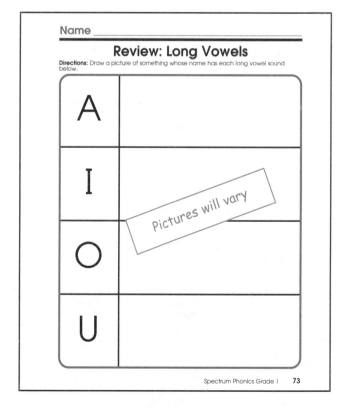

Name _____

Review: Long Vowels

Directions: Draw a picture of something whose name has each long vowel sound below.

A	
I	Pictures will vary
O	
U	

Spectrum Phonics Grade 1   73

Answer Key

Review: Long Vowels

Directions: Each picture name below has a long vowel sound. Write a sentence using each word.

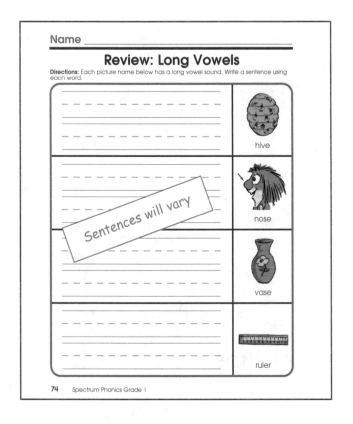

Sentences will vary

hive

nose

vase

ruler

Review: Short and Long Vowels

Directions: Say the name of each picture. Draw a line to match each picture with its name.

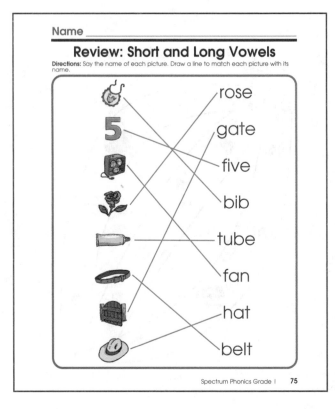

rose

gate

five

bib

tube

fan

hat

belt

Review: Short and Long Vowels

Directions: Say the name of each picture. Write the word from the Word Box that names each picture below.

bun	dive	cave	desk	
cube	milk	man	home	cob

cave   dive   desk

bun   cube   cob

man   milk   home

Review: Short and Long Vowels

Directions: Draw a picture of what each word names below.

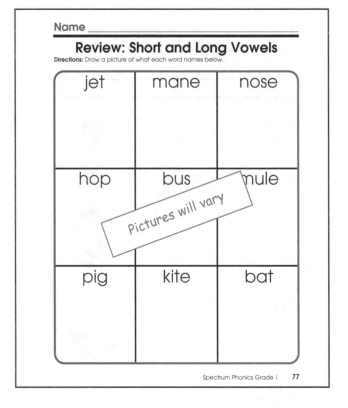

jet	mane	nose
hop	bus	mule
pig	kite	bat

Pictures will vary

Answer Key

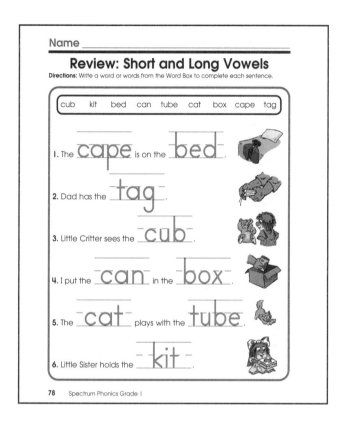

Name _____

Review: Short and Long Vowels

Directions: Write a word or words from the Word Box to complete each sentence.

> cub   kit   bed   can   tube   cat   box   cape   tag

1. The _cape_ is on the _bed_.

2. Dad has the _tag_.

3. Little Critter sees the _cub_.

4. I put the _can_ in the _box_.

5. The _cat_ plays with the _tube_.

6. Little Sister holds the _kit_.

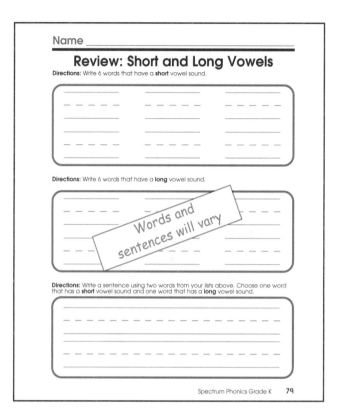

Name _____

Review: Short and Long Vowels

Directions: Write 6 words that have a **short** vowel sound.

Directions: Write 6 words that have a **long** vowel sound.

Words and sentences will vary

Directions: Write a sentence using two words from your lists above. Choose one word that has a **short** vowel sound and one word that has a **long** vowel sound.

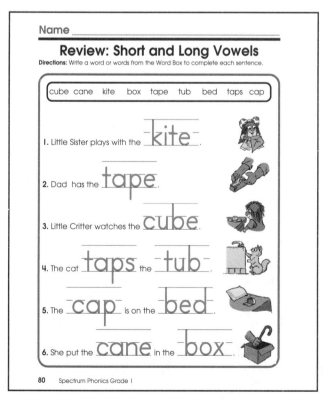

Name _____

Review: Short and Long Vowels

Directions: Write a word or words from the Word Box to complete each sentence.

> cube   cane   kite   box   tape   tub   bed   taps   cap

1. Little Sister plays with the _kite_.

2. Dad has the _tape_.

3. Little Critter watches the _cube_.

4. The cat _taps_ the _tub_.

5. The _cap_ is on the _bed_.

6. She put the _cane_ in the _box_.

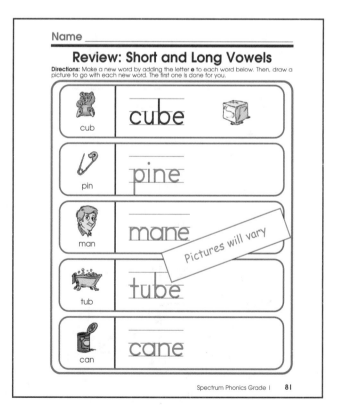

Name _____

Review: Short and Long Vowels

Directions: Make a new word by adding the letter **e** to each word below. Then, draw a picture to go with each new word. The first one is done for you.

cub	cube
pin	pine
man	mane
tub	tube
can	cane

Pictures will vary

Answer Key

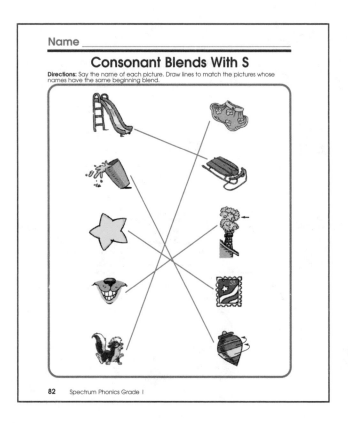

Answer Key

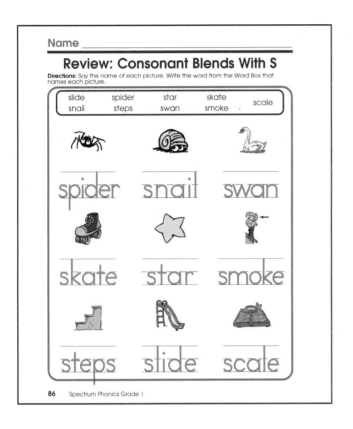

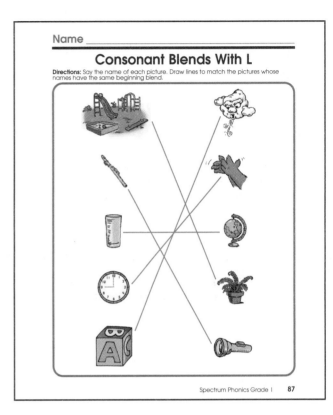

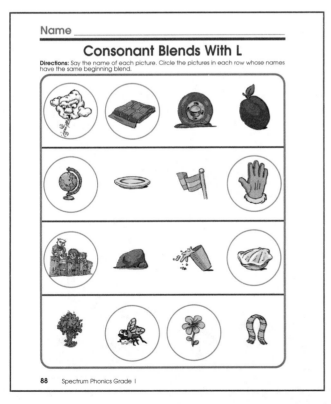

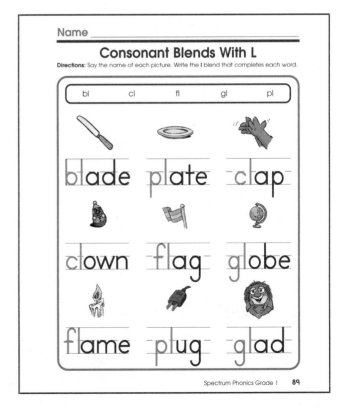

Answer Key

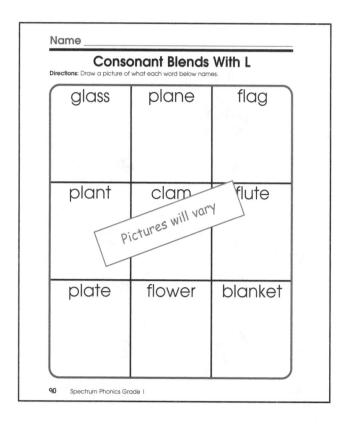

Name _____

Consonant Blends With L

Directions: Draw a picture of what each word below names.

glass	plane	flag
plant	clam	flute
plate	flower	blanket

Pictures will vary

90   Spectrum Phonics Grade 1

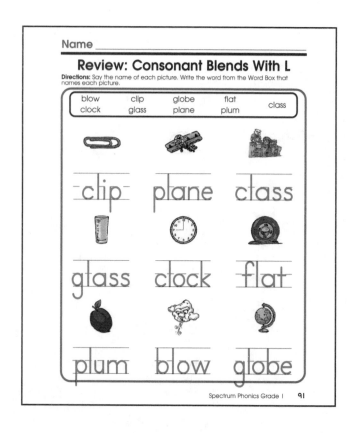

Name _____

Review: Consonant Blends With L

Directions: Say the name of each picture. Write the word from the Word Box that names each picture.

blow	clip	globe	flat	
clock	glass	plane	plum	class

clip   plane   class

glass   clock   flat

plum   blow   globe

Spectrum Phonics Grade 1   91

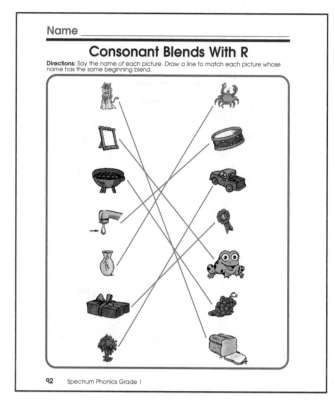

Name _____

Consonant Blends With R

Directions: Say the name of each picture. Draw a line to match each picture whose name has the same beginning blend.

92   Spectrum Phonics Grade 1

Name _____

Consonant Blends With R

Directions: Say the name of each picture. Circle the pictures in each row whose names have the same beginning blend.

Spectrum Phonics Grade 1   93

Answer Key

Answer Key

Name _____

Final Blends With S

Directions: Say the name of each picture. Write the final **s** blend that completes each word.

sk	st

crust   vest   cast

desk   list   tusk

mask   fist   chest

98   Spectrum Phonics Grade 1

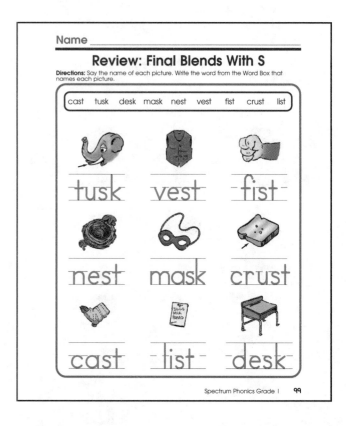

Name _____

Review: Final Blends With S

Directions: Say the name of each picture. Write the word from the Word Box that names each picture.

cast   tusk   desk   mask   nest   vest   fist   crust   list

tusk   vest   fist

nest   mask   crust

cast   fist   desk

Spectrum Phonics Grade 1   99

Name _____

Review: Consonant Blends

Directions: Say the name of each picture. Write the word from the Word Box that names each picture.

flag   smoke   plate   skirt   stamp
broom   club   slide   grapes

club   smoke   flag

grapes   plate   skirt

stamp   broom   slide

100   Spectrum Phonics Grade 1

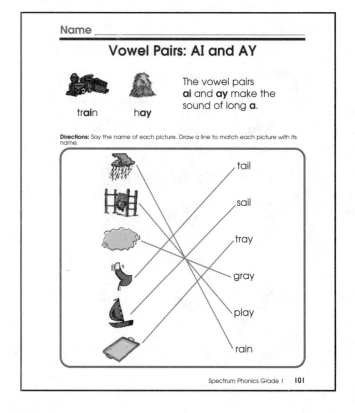

Name _____

Vowel Pairs: AI and AY

train   hay

The vowel pairs **ai** and **ay** make the sound of long **a**.

Directions: Say the name of each picture. Draw a line to match each picture with its name.

tail

sail

tray

gray

play

rain

Spectrum Phonics Grade 1   101

Answer Key

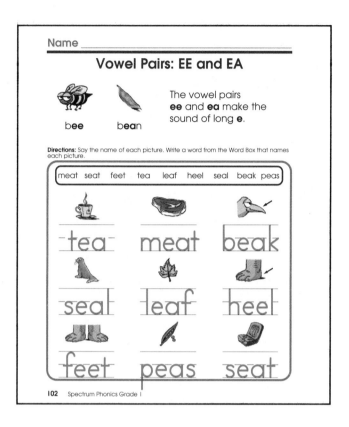

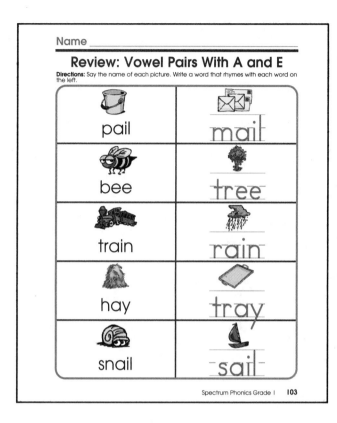

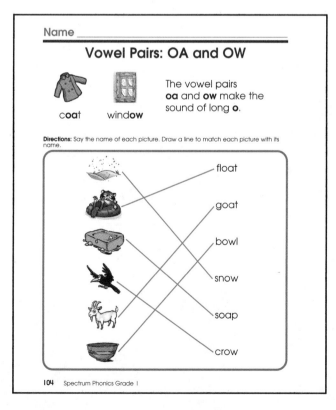

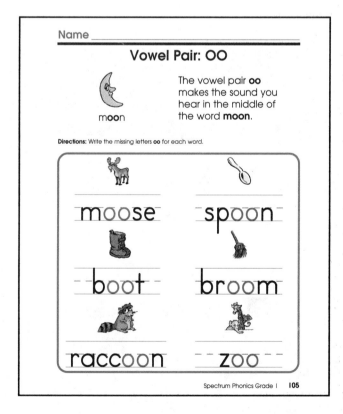

Answer Key

Name _____
Vowel Pair: OO

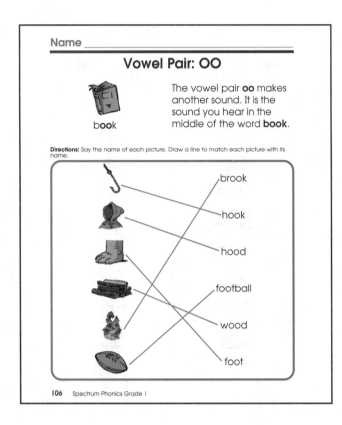

book

The vowel pair **oo** makes another sound. It is the sound you hear in the middle of the word **book**.

Directions: Say the name of each picture. Draw a line to match each picture with its name.

- brook
- hook
- hood
- football
- wood
- foot

Name _____
Vowel Pair: OO

Directions: Each of the words below have the vowel pair **oo**. Draw a picture to go with each word.

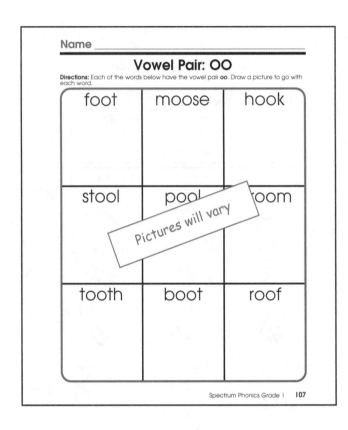

foot	moose	hook
stool	pool	room
tooth	boot	roof

Pictures will vary

Name _____
Review: Vowel Pairs With OA, OO, OW

Directions: Say the name of each picture. Write the word from the Word Box that names each picture.

food	foot	woods	moon	
soap	pool	bowl	crow	toad

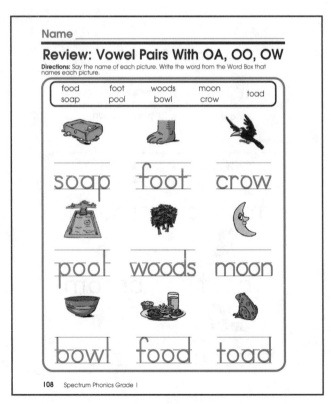

soap   foot   crow

pool   woods   moon

bowl   food   toad

Name _____
Y as Long i

fly

In some words, the letter **y** has the long **i** sound.

Directions: Name each picture and write the word from the Word Box. Then, write two sentences. Use one word from the Word Box in each sentence.

cry	fry	fly	sky

fly   cry

sky   fry

1. _____

Sentences will vary

2. _____

Answer Key

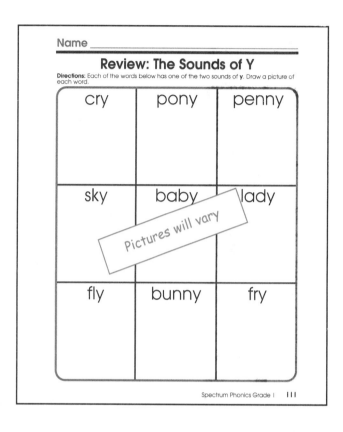

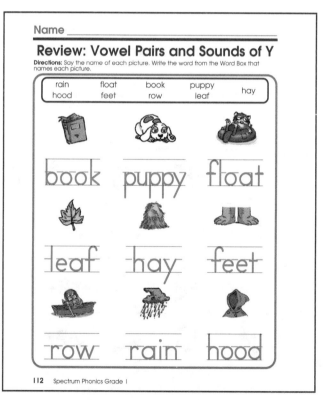

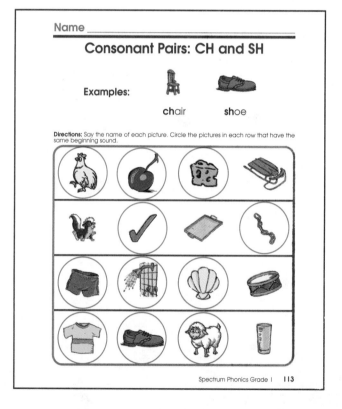

Answer Key

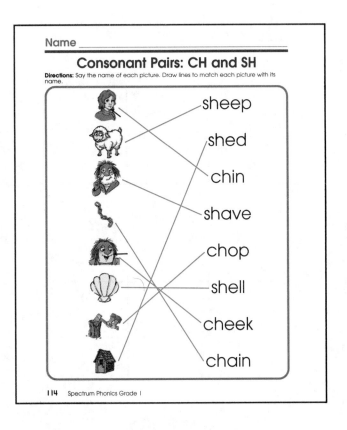

Name _____

Consonant Pairs: CH and SH

Directions: Say the name of each picture. Draw lines to match each picture with its name.

sheep

shed

chin

shave

chop

shell

cheek

chain

114   Spectrum Phonics Grade 1

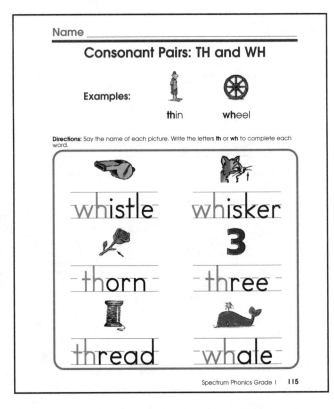

Name _____

Consonant Pairs: TH and WH

Examples:

thin   wheel

Directions: Say the name of each picture. Write the letters **th** or **wh** to complete each word.

whistle   whisker

thorn   three

thread   whale

Spectrum Phonics Grade 1   115

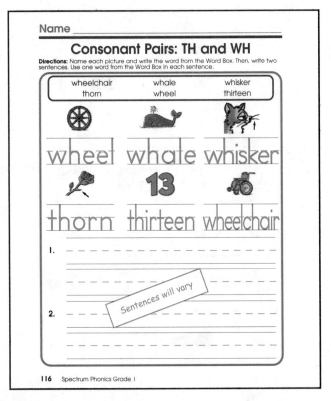

Name _____

Consonant Pairs: TH and WH

Directions: Name each picture and write the word from the Word Box. Then, write two sentences. Use one word from the Word Box in each sentence.

| wheelchair | whale | whisker |
| thorn | wheel | thirteen |

wheel   whale   whisker

thorn   thirteen wheelchair

1. _____

2. _____

Sentences will vary

116   Spectrum Phonics Grade 1

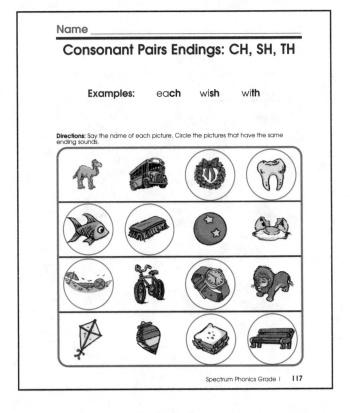

Name _____

Consonant Pairs Endings: CH, SH, TH

Examples: each   wish   with

Directions: Say the name of each picture. Circle the pictures that have the same ending sounds.

Spectrum Phonics Grade 1   117

Answer Key

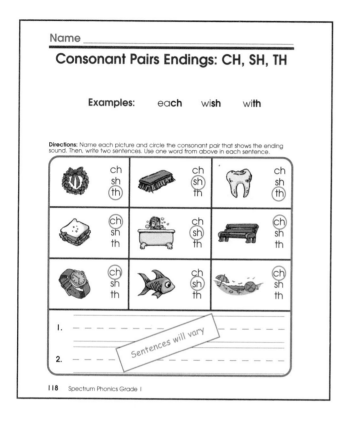

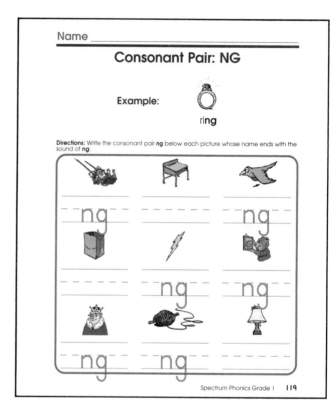

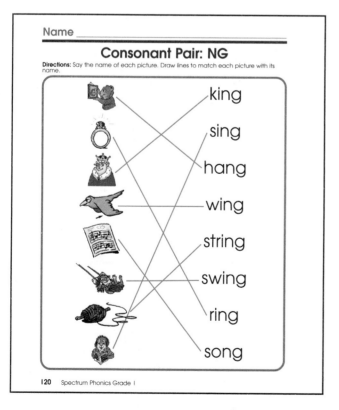

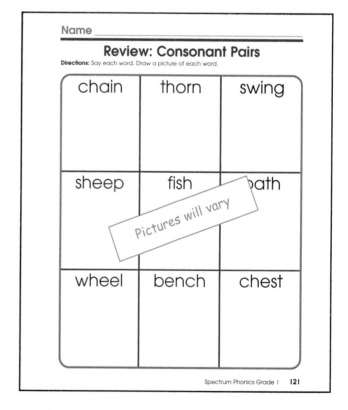

Answer Key

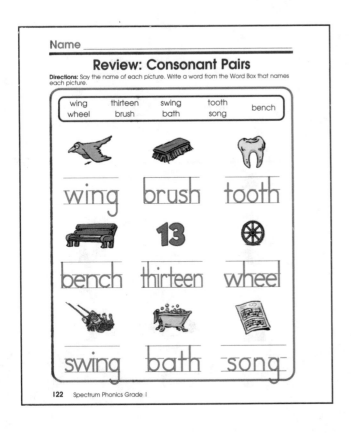

Name _____

Review: Consonant Pairs

Directions: Say the name of each picture. Write a word from the Word Box that names each picture.

wing	thirteen	swing	tooth	
wheel	brush	bath	song	bench

wing   brush   tooth

bench   thirteen   wheel

swing   bath   song

122   Spectrum Phonics Grade 1

Notes

Notes